TOWERS OF STRENGTH

- Billy Pitt had them built, Buck Mulligan said,
when the French were on the sea.

James Joyce, Ulysses *('Telemachus')*

To Liz

TOWERS OF STRENGTH

The Story of the Martello Towers

W H CLEMENTS

LEO COOPER

First published in 1999 by
LEO COOPER
an imprint of
Pen Sword Books Limited
47 Church Street, Barnsley, South Yorkshire S70 2AS

Copyright ©

ISBN 0 85052 679 5

A CIP catalogue of this book is available
from the British Library

Printed by Redwood Books Limited
Trowbridge, Wiltshire

*For up-to-date information on other titles produced under the Leo Cooper imprint, please
telephone or write to:*
Pen & Sword Books Ltd, FREEPOST, 47 Church Street
Barnsley, South Yorkshire S70 2AS
Telephone 01226 734222

Contents

ACKNOWLEDGEMENTS 6

PREFACE 9

INTRODUCTION 10

1. THE DESIGN OF THE MARTELLO TOWER 17

2. THE ENGLISH SOUTH AND EAST COAST DEFENCES 29

3. THE FATE OF THE ENGLISH TOWERS 37

4. THE SPANISH AND THE MINORCAN TOWERS 48

5. THE TOWERS IN IRELAND 59

6. THE CHANNEL ISLANDS AND SCOTLAND 83

7. CANADA 1796 TO 1815 95

8. THE DEFENCE OF EMPIRE 105

9. THE FINAL TOWERS 128

10. THE TOWERS THAT NEVER WERE 145

11. THE AMERICAN TOWERS 154

CONCLUSION 162

ANNEX A. MARTELLO TOWERS REMAINING IN
GREAT BRITAIN, IRELAND AND THE CHANNEL ISLANDS 165

ANNEX B. SMOOTH-BORE GUNS, HOWITZERS
AND MORTARS IN USE IN THE BRITISH ARMY
BETWEEN 1795 AND 1825 172

NOTES 174

BIBLIOGRAPHY 181

GLOSSARY 184

INDEX 187

Acknowledgements

My interest in Martello towers really stems from 1966 when I was stationed at the School of Infantry at Hythe in Kent. With towers on the rifle ranges, and in Shorncliffe Camp, and with the Dymchurch Redoubt still used by the Army I was intrigued to learn more about these handsome structures. The opportunity to research and write about them came only with my retirement from the Army in 1992; since then I have been able to visit all the towers in England, Wales, Ireland and Jersey. Abroad I have travelled to see the towers in Key West in Florida and in India I found the one remaining tower of those built as part of the fortifications of Old Delhi.

However, without the help of many friends, acquaintances and even total strangers the research for this book could never have been completed, nor many of the photographs acquired. Indeed, I have been so amazed at the help and encouragement I have received from so many people that it would be difficult, if not wellnigh impossible, to mention all of them by name without these acknowledgements becoming a book in themselves.

Of those whom I must acknowledge the closest to home, so to speak, is my brother-in-law Campbell Morrison, for his advice and help with word-processing and for his help in enhancing a number of the photographs, and my nephews Sebastian and Yatelyn McBride. Sebastian obtained photographs of the Leith tower while Yatelyn obtained copies of articles for me from the Library of Trinity College Dublin. Michael Pugh, an Australian professional photographer, prepared the maps and the comparative plans and sections of the English, Irish and Channel Islands towers and took photographs of Fort Denison in Sydney Harbour. An old friend from my time in Peking, John Maclennan, photographed the Guernsey towers for me, walking round the island's coastline in wintery weather to obtain the pictures.

As my research developed it soon became apparent that Martello towers were much more widespread than I had at first realized. They were not limited to the United Kingdom, the Channel Islands and Ireland. It was at this point that I received willing assistance from organizations and individuals all over the world. Dr Monique Koenig and Phillipe Lahausse de Lalouvriere of the Mauritius Friends of the Environment provided information and pictures of towers on Mauritius, while Pauline Lafford of the Halifax Defence Complex,

Marie Cantin of the National Battlefields Commission in Quebec, and Professor J.G.Pike of the Royal Military College in Kingston, Ontario, provided virtually all my information on and pictures of the Canadian towers.

I am particularly grateful to another old friend and colleague Colonel Jeremy Dumas who, while Defence Adviser at the British High Commission in Kingston, Jamaica, found time to photograph the towers at Fort Nugent in Jamaica and Fort Picton in Trinidad. Other military officers to whom I also owe a debt of gratitude are Commandant Peter Young of the Military Archives in Dublin, Colonel Francisco Fornalls Villalonga, Director of the Military Museum in Mahon, Minorca, and Lieutenant-Colonel Tim O'Donnell, Defence Adviser at the British High Commission, Colombo.

I also wish to thank Dr Edward Harris of the Bermuda Maritime Museum for providing a copy of his article on the tower at Ferry Point published in the *Mariner's Mirror* and photographs of the tower. Desmond Nicholson of the Antigua and Barbuda Museum provided plans of River Fort on Barbuda, and Mr C.T.Henry, Assistant Curator at the Royal Armouries, Fort Nelson, was particularly patient and painstaking in providing answers to my questions about eighteenth- and nineteenth-century smooth-bore artillery. My thanks also go to Ruth Mateer for her help in translating material on the towers in Sicily from the original Italian, and to Greg Cox for the drawings of the Gando tower and River Fort, Barbuda.

I have corresponded with Brian Pegden for almost two years and I have to thank him for the suggested title of this book and also for reading the first draft and suggesting a number of corrections and amendments. I found his introduction to the published material on Martello towers invaluable in pointing me in the direction of a number of them which previously I had not known to exist, including that at Fort Beaufort in South Africa. Further details concerning this tower and a photograph came from Brian Jackson of the Grahamstown office of the National Monuments Council for South Africa. My thanks also go to Peter Hibbs who has compiled a most instructive database on the Kent and Sussex towers; to Crown and Company of Cardiff for providing me with the sales particulars of Stack Rock Fort from their records; and to Sue Hardy of the National Trust for Jersey for details of the Victoria Tower.

A special debt of gratitude is owed by me to Professor Hiro Bulchand of Las Palmas, Gran Canaria. He provided a translation of a booklet on the Gando Tower and, thanks to his dogged perseverence and by making use of his friends and acquaintances in Las Palmas, he obtained photographs of the tower despite its being sited inside a restricted military area. Others to whom my thanks must go for their help are Nigel Hankin for introducing me to the tower in Delhi; John Goodwin for the details of the towers on the Scilly Isles (which were not, after all, Martello towers); to Phil Brooks of the Ascension Heritage Society; to Mary Billot, Librarian of the Société Jersiaise; to Margaret Pinsent of the Fortress Study Group; and to Charlotte Haslam, lately Architectural Adviser to the Landmark Trust, who died suddenly and tragically in early 1997.

These acknowledgements would not be complete without reference and thanks to the staff of the Public Record Office at Kew, the Royal Engineers Library at Chatham, the Kent County Council Centre for Kentish Studies, the British Library, the National Army Museum, the Biblioteca Centrale della Regione Siciliana, and the Austrian State Archives for their unstinting help and advice. Without the records which these bodies maintain so professionally this book could never have been written.

My final thanks go to my wife Liz. For thirty years or more all over the world, from the Channel Islands to China, America to Australia, she has clambered over fortifications in all weathers with me. The fact that this book has been successfully completed is entirely due to her support, encouragement and skill with the computer, and it is for these reasons that it is dedicated to her.

Preface

When I started to write this book I was faced with the task of setting its parameters. What is a Martello tower? Which of the many towers built by the British Army should be included and which excluded? Sheila Sutcliffe in her own book on them believed that the essential characteristics of these towers should include a massive wall, a flat roof and a door and an entrance passage raised above the ground, usually at first-floor level. To some people only the towers on the southern and the eastern coast of England can properly be termed 'Martello' towers; but even here there is a problem of definition since there are two distinct designs, one in use in Kent and Sussex and the other in Essex and Suffolk. Indeed, the design of the early nineteenth-century towers does seem to reflect the training, experience and even individual whims of each Royal Engineer officer in charge of their construction.

On the whole I have accepted Sutcliffe's definition but I have gone beyond the purist's concept of only elliptical or cam-shaped towers being classified as Martello towers. I have decided to include all the later ones which are referred to in Board of Ordnance estimates of the time as Martello towers, a term which by the mid-nineteenth century was generic for gun-towers of almost any shape. I have, however, excluded 'defensible guardhouses', blockhouses and the square or circular keeps sometimes found in the later Victorian forts.

I have included the smaller Jersey and Guernsey towers, and accepted the late William Davies's suggestion that they should be called 'Conway' towers, since they are almost of the same period and were the immediate precursors of the Martello towers. Only in the case of the towers at Delhi have I perhaps taken something of a liberty. Once again the fortification purists may say with justification that these towers are really circular bastions. However, the British engineer officers of the Mutiny called them Martello towers in their journals and memoirs, and so I have included them.

This book is a general description of most of the Martello towers built by the British in Britain, Ireland and elsewhere throughout the world, and I have also followed Sutcliffe's lead in including a short account of similar towers built in the United States. However, the book does not attempt to be an exhaustive study of the history of their construction, but I hope that it will inform and interest anyone who wishes to know more about these fascinating fortifications.

W.H.C. London, 1998

Introduction

Throughout history the south-east coast of England has always been considered the part of the country most vulnerable to an enemy invasion. In Roman times the Count of the Saxon Shore commanded nine forts situated between the Wash and Portchester to defend the Roman province from attack by Saxon raiders, and in the Middle Ages the Cinque Ports furnished ships and money to defend the kingdom. These walled and fortified towns withstood a number of French attacks, but it was Henry VIII who ordered the building of the ten 'Great Castles' between Deal and Falmouth, providing the first coastal artillery defences against an invader. Of these ten 'Castles' the four largest, Deal, Walmer, Sandgate and Camber, were sited to defend Kent, the corner of England closest to France.

The threat of invasion appeared again during the Napoleonic Wars and it was in the years 1803 to 1805 that this threat forced the British government to review the defences of the south and the east coast of England. A scheme was put forward in 1803 by Captain W.H. Ford to Brigadier General Twiss, Commanding Engineer of the Southern District, for a chain of towers, mounting guns, along the Kent and the Sussex coast. This line of towers, close to beaches and possible landing places, was designed to protect the coast between Folkestone and Eastbourne.

The use of outlying defensive towers to protect fortified places was by no means a new concept in 1803. Almost fifty years earlier Marshal Saxe, the famous French commander, had recommended a line of towers to protect a fortified town or citadel. Saxe, writing in his *Reveries, or Memoirs upon the Art of War,* published in London in 1757, suggested the erection of a series of advanced towers around the principal fortified work, believing them to be superior to redoubts which required large numbers of troops to garrison them. So the use of towers either as outworks or as keeps was well known to the engineer officers of the day. Towers were also commonly used to defend vulnerable beaches and harbours along the shores of the Mediterranean; on Corsica, where they were known as 'Genoese towers'; in the Balearic Islands and further afield on the Canary Islands. On the Italian coast these towers were known as 'Saracen towers' and many were used as watch or signal towers to warn of the approach of corsairs or other pirates.

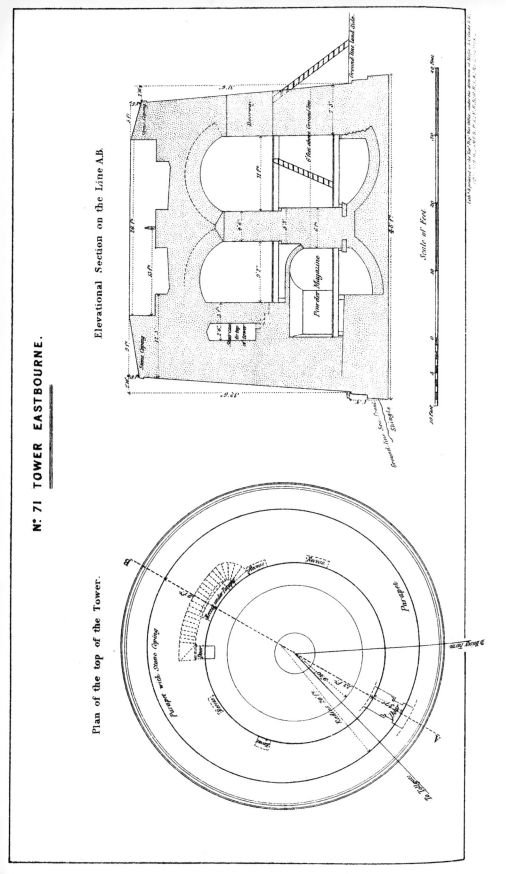

Nº 71 TOWER EASTBOURNE.

Elevational Section on the Line A,B.

Powder Magazine

Plan of the top of the Tower.

Parapet with Stone Coping

Parapet

Scale of Feet

Plan and section of a south-coast tower (No.71). [PRO WO 33/9]

In 1794 elements of the British Mediterranean fleet which was blockading Corsica attacked one such tower at Mortella Point in the Bay of San Fiorenzo in the north of the island. Admiral Lord Howe, always opposed to a purely passive blockade, had decided upon offensive action to destroy the tower and despatched a landing force under the command of Major-General Dundas to Mortella Bay. Two Royal Navy ships, HMS *Fortitude* (74 guns) and HMS *Juno* (32 guns), bombarded the tower for over two hours and, despite the tower's being armed only with two 18pdr and a small 6pdr gun, or, as other sources maintain, two 12pdr guns, both ships were driven off with considerable loss but with little damage having been done to the tower. It was only after troops had been landed and field artillery used to bombard the tower that it was eventually captured, only to be finally destroyed when the British withdrew from the island in 1796.

It was the ability of the tower at Mortella Point to withstand naval attack which almost certainly led to the construction by the British of eleven such on Minorca when they held the island from 1798 to 1802. These towers followed the design of two Spanish towers which were already part of the island's defences. It was because the design of these towers was considered by a number of senior British officers to be so successful from both a military and an economic point of view that further towers were built in England and Ireland, and these came to be commonly known as Martello towers.

There has been considerable discussion over the years concerning the derivation of the name 'Martello'. The most commonly accepted explanation is that it was derived from the reputation of the tower at Mortella Point and is simply a corruption of the name which, bearing in mind the British serviceman's ability to adopt and modify foreign words, does seem quite likely. An alternative suggestion, however, is that the name comes from Torri di Martello (Hammer Towers), built on the Italian coast. Some sources suggest these towers were called hammer towers because of the warning bell on the top of each which was sounded by striking the bell with a hammer. Other sources maintain that the towers, with their machicolation, were so named because when viewed from a distance they appeared in outline to resemble a hammer. Whatever the derivation, and the most generally held view is the first one given above, the word 'Martello' is now the generic term used to describe British nineteenth-century gun towers.

It is difficult to identify the first Martello tower to be built in Britain or Ireland. Three were designed locally in Guernsey and construction began in 1804 on the orders of the island's Lieutenant Governor, Major-General Doyle, but by September 1805 they were still incom-

The tower at Mortella Point, St. Fiorenza Bay, Corsica, from a contemporary aquatint.
[National Maritime Museum]

plete. In Ireland Colonel Twiss had been brought over to carry out a
survey of the defences in 1803 and his report had resulted in the
construction of towers on Bere and Garinish Islands in Bantry Bay,
while other towers had been proposed by the Commander-in-Chief
in Ireland for the defence of Dublin, including the construction of
towers north and south of the city.[1] The Bere Island towers were
completed by February 1805 and the Dublin towers by December of
the same year. Therefore it would seem that some of the Irish towers
may be said to be the earliest to be planned and constructed.
However, what is also clear is that in the period from 1803 to 1805
the idea of towers for coastal defence was current in English engineer
thinking and Captain Ford, in suggesting such towers for the defence
of the English south coast, was simply propounding a standard solution for the problem. The main difference in this case was the scale of
the scheme and the fact that it came at a time of national crisis when
the authorities were prepared to expend the large sums of money
necessary to implement it.

The proposal to build a line of towers along the Kent and the Sussex coast required the authority of the Board of Ordnance before it could be implemented. The Board was one of the three departments subordinate to the Secretary of State for War and the Colonies who administered the Army at that time. (The other two were the old War Office, under the Secretary *at* War, and the Commander-in-Chief at the Horse Guards, an appointment established in 1793, who commanded the cavalry and the infantry, together with field armies.)

The Board of Ordnance was the body responsible for approving and constructing all permanent fortifications and barracks, as well as providing weapons and munitions for both the Army and the Royal Navy. In many ways it was similar to the Board of Admiralty, having both civilian and military members. The chairman of the Board was the Master General of the Ordnance who was also a member of the Privy Council and, as such, was the government's principal military adviser. Thus he wielded considerable political as well as military authority, and his office approved all financial estimates and paid for the construction and repair of fortifications, from a budget separate from the funds allotted by Parliament to the Commander-in-Chief for the maintenance of the Army.

Although the ultimate authority for all decisions on fortifications lay, in fact, with the Secretary for War and the Colonies, this was really a formality. By 1800 the Master General was always a senior Army officer and it had become difficult for the Secretary for War, as a civilian, to disregard his views, particularly given the Master General's political position. So the Board of Ordnance, which was aided by a subordinate committee responsible for advice on all fortifications (the Committee of Engineers), usually had the final say in all such matters, particularly when such powerful political figures as the Earl of Chatham, William Pitt's elder brother, and the Duke of Wellington held the post of Master General.

The third most senior soldier on the Board, after the Lieutenant General of the Ordnance, was the Inspector General of Fortifications, the senior engineer officer in the armed forces. He commanded the three professional corps, the Royal Artillery, the Royal Engineers and the Royal Sappers and Miners. To the office of the Inspector General was delegated the task of drawing up all plans and budgets for the construction and repair of fortifications, barracks and other works, and he was also responsible for the supervision of the work. No work on permanent fortifications could be begun without the Board's authorization but on occasions, and in order to speed up construction, this procedure could be circumvented by commanders who would describe the proposed fortifications as 'field works', so permitting the use of funds disbursed by the Headquarters at the Horse Guards.

While it was the Board of Ordnance which approved plans and provided money for permanent fortifications, it was the officers of the Royal Engineers who initiated the designs and supervised the construction. In 1805 the Corps of Royal Engineers comprised only 121 officers and 37 surveyors and draughtsmen, though this total had doubled by 1815. In each military district, division or colony there was a commanding engineer responsible for all Board of Ordnance works, usually with one or more junior officers to assist him. Overseas the construction of fortifications was only one aspect of the public works which the commanding engineer was responsible for. In Canada and India Royal Engineers officers built canals, on Ascension Island an officer seconded to the Admiralty designed the island's water supply and its hospital, and everywhere British troops were stationed the Royal Engineers designed and built their barracks. Comparatively junior officers had considerable financial responsibility and lieutenants and captain-lieutenants supervised local contractors, ensuring that no defective materials were used or slipshod building methods permitted.

The scheme for towers proposed by Captain Ford was different since they were to stand alone and unsupported by batteries. The Committee of Engineers believed that towers should be used to provide a keep for a battery and were of the opinion that towers on their own and supported only by other towers some distance away would provide no advantage over a battery other than a defence against infantry assault.[2] However, many of the officers involved in the expedition to Corsica and who knew of the action in Mortella Bay subsequently achieved high rank and positions of influence in military planning. By 1803 General Dundas was commanding Southern District, covering the section of the English coast most threatened by invasion. Lieutenant-Colonel Nepean, RE, another officer who had accompanied the Corsican expedition, was a member of the Committee of Engineers. So when Ford's plan was submitted by Twiss to the Board there were a number of officers influentially placed to support it.

It was fifteen months before the plan for towers along the south coast was eventually accepted by the Board of Ordnance and building commenced in 1805, after the threat of invasion had actually diminished. The line, comprising seventy-four towers, was complete by 1810 and now extended as far as Seaford near Newhaven, though no towers were built along the stretch of coastline between Eastbourne and the final tower at Seaford. In 1805 a further proposal to protect the east coast was approved and a second line of twenty-nine towers, extending from Clacton in Essex to Aldeburgh in Suffolk, was constructed between 1809 and 1812. The towers in Kent and Sussex were numbered 1 to 74, starting with No.1 on The Warren at Folkestone, and ending with No. 74 at Seaford. The tower of Sandgate Castle, one of Henry VIII's 'Great Castles', was converted into a Martello tower but was not given a number. The towers in Essex and Suffolk were not numbered but, instead, identified by letter: A to Z with the last three referred to as AA, BB and CC, or sometimes as A2, B2 and C2.

Martello tower building continued after the completion of the English east-coast towers with further examples in Scotland, Ireland, Canada, Sicily and the Adriatic before the war ended in 1815. Although the end of the war reduced the scale of fortification building such building never actually ceased. There was always a need for fortifications to defend the colonies and, among other places, towers were built in Bermuda, Mauritius and South Africa. The final ones, much larger than the original towers, were completed in the 1850s, just as the new rifled ordnance was coming into service and making masonry fortifications obsolete.

The English Martello towers never saw action, although it is believed that in the Second World War the North East Martello Tower at Pembroke Dock engaged German bombers with Lewis guns mounted on the gun platform, and the majority of the towers were disarmed and abandoned before the end of the nineteenth century. During the Second World War some were used as observation posts and for beach defence, and today, although many are derelict, a number of those remaining have been converted into private residences or holiday homes. The rest, however, have an uncertain future and it is to be hoped that their historical value will be recognized so that funds may be made available to halt their decline into dereliction and enable the necessary essential maintenance to be carried out.

CHAPTER 1

The Design of the Martello Tower

The term 'Martello tower' has become a generic one for coast defence towers which were built in Britain and the Empire between 1796 and 1860. There are a number of different designs for these towers, but it is those that were built along the south and the east coast of England which are considered to be true Martello towers.

The essential features of a true Martello tower were that it was a circular masonry structure mounting one or a number of guns on the terreplein, or roof area. It normally had a bomb-proof arch above its second floor covered in masonry up to the terreplein, the whole being supported by a massive, central pillar. There was always just a single door usually at first-floor level and a number of towers were surrounded by a ditch.

The external appearance of a typical tower resembled an inverted plant pot with a 'batter' to the walls, that is, the diameter of the tower at the parapet level was less than that at the base, causing the walls to slope inwards towards the top of the tower. The average height of the towers was usually 30 to 35ft (9.2 to 10m), and most were elliptical

Tower 73 (the Wish Tower) on the seafront at Eastbourne. [Author's photograph]

in shape with a diameter at the base of between 40 and 50ft (12.3 to 15.3m) and at the parapet of between 35 and 40ft (10.75 to 12.3m).

The later east-coast towers were larger than those in Kent and Sussex and were cam-shaped rather than elliptical. Although their height was similar, the east-coast towers had a much greater diameter and the broadest part of the base averaged 55ft (16.9m). In both the south- and the east-coast towers the front section of the wall, facing the sea, was thicker than the section at the rear in order to present a stronger defence to an enemy bombardment. Such was the scale of the tower building programme in 1805, and the urgency of construction, that it was necessary to use a number of contractors and sub-contractors and this, in turn, led to slight differences between the towers, particularly in their dimensions. On average, the width of the front section of the wall at the base was about 13ft (4m) diminishing to 9ft (2.7m) at the top. The rear section was thinner, the width being reduced to 7ft (2m) at the base and 5ft (1.5m) at the top. The terreplein, or gun platform, at the top of the tower was made of brick coped with stone, with an average diameter of 26ft (8m), and there were recesses in the parapet wall to hold the ready ammunition.

On the south and the east coast a total of twenty-two towers were surrounded by a dry ditch, including Towers 4 to 9 which were situated along the cliff edge from The Leas at Folkestone to Shorncliffe, Towers 28, 29 and 30 at Rye, Towers 43, 44, 68 and 73 between Rye and Eastbourne, and Tower 74 at Seaford . The ditch at Tower 28, the tower at Rye Harbour, which was built on loose shingle, had a buttressed brick counterscarp supporting the shingle piled against it to form a low raised embankment, or glacis. This wall can be seen today now that the shingle has disappeared, and a similar wall is visible in front of Tower 74 at Seaford. The towers on the east coast provided with ditches were: Tower F at Clacton-on-Sea, J at Walton-on-the-Naze, L at Shotley Gate, N at Walton Ferry, P, Q and R at Felixstowe and CC at Aldeburgh.

The towers at Seaford and Aldeburgh stood in isolation from the remainder of the south- and the east-coast towers and therefore the added protection provided by the ditch was particularly important. The dimensions of the ditches varied considerably but averaged about 15ft (4.6m) deep with a width from the counterscarp to the tower of about 40ft (12.3m). However, the ditch around Tower N at Walton Ferry, on the banks of the River Orwell in Suffolk, was 70ft (21.5m) wide, but this was exceptionally large. Tower N also had a cunette, a subsidiary trench filled with water 20ft (6.1m) wide, constructed within the ditch. The only other tower to have a cunette was Tower 30 at Rye, but here it was considerably narrower. Three towers, Towers 68, 73 and CC, had a glacis surrounding the ditch which reduced the amount of the tower vulnerable to artillery fire.

The English towers were extremely strong, being built of brick rendered with stucco, which acted as weatherproofing and provided an unclimbable surface. On average between 250,000 and 300,000 bricks were used in each south-coast tower and half a million for the larger towers on the east coast.[1] The bricks were bonded with a mixture of lime, ash and hot tallow which set so hard that it enabled

Types of Martello tower in Britain. [Michael Pugh]

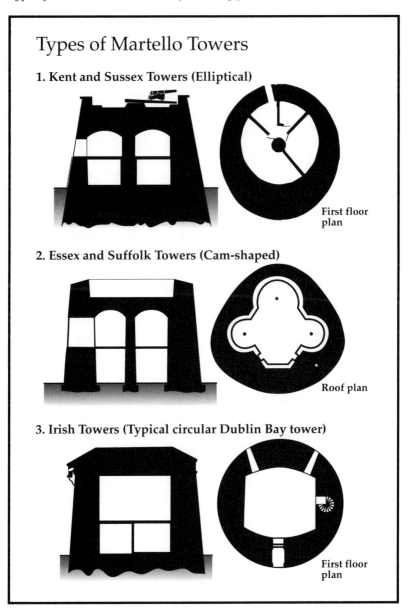

Types of Martello Towers

1. Kent and Sussex Towers (Elliptical)

First floor plan

2. Essex and Suffolk Towers (Cam-shaped)

Roof plan

3. Irish Towers (Typical circular Dublin Bay tower)

First floor plan

the towers to withstand all attempts of wind, weather and man to destroy them. Two examples serve to illustrate how difficult this was: in 1874 an experiment was carried out using gun cotton slabs to demolish Tower No.10 at Hythe in Kent; after two unsuccessful attempts the tower was finally destroyed when 200lb (90kg) of gun cotton was placed between the central pillar and the thick sea face of the wall. Secondly, in 1956, when it became necessary to remove Tower No.22 at Dymchurch in order to widen the road, it required a number of attempts by the Royal Engineers using explosives, after all mechanical methods had failed, before the tower was eventually brought down.

In Ireland and overseas there was little brick immediately available and towers were built from local materials, including rubble masonry, granite, sandstone and even black basalt ashlar. In most towers bricks were used internally, particularly for the bomb-proof arch, but an exception was the tower of Fort Denison in Sydney Harbour where the arch was built of finely crafted, sandstone ashlar.

Entry to the towers was usually through a single door at the back on the first-floor level, approached up a ladder or, in the case of the twenty-one towers surrounded by a ditch, across a small drawbridge. In the towers entered by means of a ladder there was a stone chute beneath the sill of the door to take the ladder; an iron plate with an aperture in it was fitted across the sill to allow the ladder to be pulled into the tower after the door had been closed.

The south-coast towers had two small windows, also at first-floor level, one on each side wall of the tower, enabling an unbroken wall to face the sea, while the east-coast towers, being larger, had four windows. The doorways and windows of the east-coast towers were finished with particularly fine quoined stone which was not covered with stucco and which today stands out strikingly on those towers where the wall stucco has fallen away. A number of towers, particularly those built later in the mid-nineteenth century and many overseas, had additional windows and embrasures.

Most Martello towers were built on three levels with a basement, first floor and gun platform. The basement was actually the ground floor of the tower but had no doorway and was entered by means of a ladder through a trapdoor in the floor above. In the basement were the magazine and the provision store. In the south-coast towers the magazine was partly recessed into the wall of the tower and, in order to keep the powder dry, there was a second and inner wall with ventilation slits . This was important as most towers were noted as being very damp. The door of the magazine was covered with copper as a

Types of doorway. Left: the door of Tower 23 at Dymchurch, Kent showing the chute by means of which the ladder could be drawn up into the tower; right: the doorway of Tower 5 at Folkestone; this tower was surrounded by a ditch and so the doorway is wider with holes on either side at the top for the chains supporting the drawbridge. [Author's photographs]

Two styles of window. Left: the window of Tower 7 at Shorncliffe, Kent is simple in style with a granite ledge and a plain brick surround; right: the window of Tower W at Bawdsey Cliffs, Suffolk is more elaborate with a quoined granite surround; this picture also shows the vent at the top to allow smoke to disperse. [Author's photographs]

precaution against sparks and the hinges were made of bronze. The magazine was large enough to hold 50 barrels of gunpowder but in some cases as many as 200 barrels could be stored. A report of 1818 records that the amount of ammunition held in each south-coast tower was one hundred rounds of 24pdr solid shot, twenty rounds of case shot, twenty rounds of grapeshot and twenty of common shell.[2] The case shot and the grapeshot were early forms of anti-personnel ammunition and were used effectively against infantry at ranges up to about 300yd (246m).

Also in the basement was a water tank which was filled manually, usually from a well outside the tower. In the east coast towers a hand-pump was provided to raise the water from the cistern to the first floor. In a number of towers - obviously where no well could be provided close to the tower - a drainage system leading from the gun platform to the cistern in the basement through pipes set into the wall enabled rainwater to be collected. This was the case in the Longhope Sound towers on Orkney and the later Kempt Tower on Jersey. In a few towers, including one on Minorca and one in Ireland, a well was provided inside the tower itself.

The first floor of the tower was made of wooden planks laid across oak joists which radiated from the central pillar. This was the main living area for the garrison which was one officer and twenty-four soldiers in the English towers. The first floor comprised a main room for the soldiers; a second room, only a little smaller, for the officer; and a third, small room which was the Quartermaster Sergeant's store. The ceiling of the first floor was vaulted and its immense thickness was needed to make it bomb-proof and to take the weight of the heavy gun mounted above it. In the smaller towers the bomb-proof arch often consisted of a dome supported by the circular pier formed by the exterior wall. In the larger towers the arch was supported not only by the exterior wall but also by a central, circular, brick pillar rising from the base of the tower. This was a standard feature of the English towers but a number of others built in Minorca, Ireland and Bermuda lacked a central pillar.

Access to the gun platform, or terreplein, was by a stone staircase built into the thickest part of the tower wall. In the Kent and the Sussex towers the flight of stairs ended in a small oak door, and between it and the gun platform were three further steps, the final one being the raised block on which the racer for the gun was placed. The door at the head of the stairs was kept closed when the gun was in action but there was a circular hole in the bottom of the door which was closed by means of a sliding hatch on the stairs side of it. This hole

Tower E at Clacton-on-Sea, Essex, a typical east-coast tower; the picture gives an indication of the cam shape and shows three of the four windows. [Author's photograph]

was designed to enable 24pdr solid shot and other ammunition and powder charges to be passed through to the gunners without the need to open the door. In this the English towers differed from the earlier Minorcan and Irish ones which were provided with a shaft leading into the gallery of the machicolation for the movement of ammunition and powder to the gun.

In the larger east-coast towers there were two staircases leading to the gun platform, the entrances to which were close to the two rear windows; there was also a vent above the stairs and each window to allow smoke which might gather inside the tower from the firing of the gun or muskets to dissipate. Smoke from the fireplaces was taken through flues to one or more chimneys mounted on the parapet ledge. These interfered with the full traverse of the gun and it must be assumed that in action they would, if necessary, have been knocked off in order to permit the gun to traverse.

In Ireland, where more than fifty Martello towers were built, the majority differed in some aspects of their design from the English models, particularly in being circular in shape and having the same thickness of wall all round. In this way they resembled a number of towers built a few years earlier by the British on the island of Minorca in the Mediterranean. Because brick was not easily obtained in Ireland and was expensive the Irish towers were built of granite ashlar or rubble masonry which was sometimes rendered externally with stucco. Most of them had a batter to the walls, although usually the slope was less than in the English towers, and frequently there was a machicolation over the door. Many of these towers were built in conjunction with a gun battery, thus forming a small fort with the tower acting as a keep or place of last defence against an infantry attack.

Martello towers were designed to mount at least one gun. The English south-coast towers were armed with one 24pdr gun mounted on a traversing platform and, in addition, eighteen towers, including Nos.1 to 9 at Folkestone and Shorncliffe and nine in Sussex, were shown in a return of 1818 as having one $5\frac{1}{2}$in iron howitzer on charge.[3] In the original proposal for the construction of the towers it had been planned to mount two carronades on specially designed mountings in addition to the 24pdr gun. However, it proved physically impossible to mount the carronades as well as the gun so it was then proposed that twenty-six towers should be equipped with one howitzer in place of the carronades. This number was reduced to the nine along the coast at Folkestone; the howitzer was provided specifically for the defence of the tower carrying it, since it could be approached by an enemy force over broken ground which could not be reached by fire from the 24pdr gun. Subsequently the total number

The original 24pdr gun on Tower 24 at Dymchurch, Kent; the gun has been restored by English Heritage and mounted on a reproduction traversing carriage. [Author's photograph]

was increased to eighteen with the supply of howitzers to nine of the Sussex towers.

Because it was not possible to mount the planned armament of three guns on each of the south-coast towers, those built on the east coast were designed to be larger, each supporting one 24pdr heavy gun and either two 5¹/₂in howitzers or two 24pdr carronades. These guns were mounted on a quatrefoil-shaped gun platform within the cam-shaped parapet. There was one exception: Tower CC at Aldeburgh, which, because the whole tower was quatrefoil-shaped, mounted four 24pdr guns. A number of Irish towers, being larger than the English ones, mounted two or three guns, and the design of the towers built to protect Dublin Bay and some other Irish examples provided for a furnace set into the wall of the parapet which was used to heat 18pdr or 24pdr shot.

The traversing platform on which the gun was mounted consisted of two balks of timber each 16ft (4.9m) long held together by three crosspieces, with a pair of small iron wheels fitted under the front crosspiece, and with a second pair at the rear on two legs, which raised the platform to an angle of about 20 degrees. The front wheels ran on a metal track, or racer, laid along a narrow stone ledge built at the base of the parapet wall, while the rear wheels ran along a similar track, but one with a much narrower diameter, which encircled a metal pivot and was mounted on a circular masonry block. A long gun mounted on a traversing platform required an interior space of about 20ft (6.15m) in diameter within the parapet to be able to traverse freely in all directions. A carronade or lighter gun required about 16ft (4.9m).

The pivot was frequently just an iron spike secured in the muzzle of an old, unserviceable gun barrel which was embedded upright in the centre of the gun platform. This use of a gun barrel was an economical way of ensuring that the pivot could be raised to a height which gave the traversing platform an incline from front to rear of between 10 and 20 degrees and was also strong enough to support both the weight of the platform and the gun. The gun itself was mounted on a garrison carriage on the traversing platform and the incline of the platform reduced the recoil of the gun when it was fired. The traversing platform was moved by using ropes through metal rings fixed to the inside wall of the parapet, and on the south-coast towers the platform could be turned quite easily through 360 degrees.

Where two guns were mounted by the use of a single pivot this was done by attaching the rear of each traversing platform to the pivot by means of an L-shaped bracket. On the east-coast towers, however, where three guns were mounted, there were three separate pivots and

The gun platform of Tower Z at Bawdsey, Suffolk showing two of the three unserviceable gun barrels used as pivots for the traversing platforms. [Author's photograph]

the interior of the gun platform was quatrefoil-shaped with three large gun positions each limited to a traverse of about 120 degrees. Some towers built later, and mostly overseas, had the gun mounted on a central pivot traversing platform. These platforms had the two pairs of wheels each running on the track on the ledge at the base of the parapet wall, or, in the case of a tower in Bermuda, along a track laid on a raised masonry plinth built in the centre of the platform, and were used where the diameter of the gun platform was relatively small.

All the English towers had a flag pole on the gun platform which fitted into a recess in the parapet wall. Contemporary engravings show the south-coast towers flying the Union flag, but by 1810, once the threat of invasion had passed, the towers were used as signal stations to relay simple messages between Eastbourne and Hythe by hoisting a combination of the Union flag and three black canvas balls on the flag pole.[4] A supply of such balls was delivered to the Sussex towers in October 1810 and a simple code was devised by the commanding officer of the 11th Royal Veteran Battalion, the unit responsible for the manning of the Sussex towers at that time. Tower No. 44 at Galley Hill had an Admiralty signal post built beside it in 1810.

In 1820 the Admiralty set up a chain of semaphore stations between Deal and Beachy Head, using the two-arm Popham semaphore, and incorporated five Martello towers in the chain: Tower 4 on The Leas at Folkestone, Tower 27 at Dymchurch, Tower 31 west of Rye, Tower 44 at Petts Level and Tower 55 at Normans Bay near Pevensey. It would be more correct to say that it was the Ordnance ground at each location which was used rather than the towers themselves, since the Board of Ordnance would permit semaphores to be set up only as long as they did not 'interfere with the defence at either of the stations whether the Redoubt Batteries or in the vicinity of the Martello towers' and that 'in the vicinity of the Martello towers the buildings to be erected might be any form or size provided they are not composed of either brick or stone, as nothing will be allowed to stand, in time of war, which could offer shelter to an enemy'.[5] At all five towers the semaphore mast was placed between 20 and 50yd (18.4 and 46.1m) away from the tower and signallers were accommodated in peacetime either in the towers or nearby.

In Ireland work on an an elaborate chain of stone signal towers had already been started in 1804. This was complete by 1806 and covered almost all of the coastline except for a section in the north and east between Londonderry and Dublin, where an enemy naval threat was considered to be minimal. Two Martello towers were included in the chain with the dual role of signal station and gun-tower. One of these was at Fort Point at the entrance to Rosslare Harbour and the other on Baginbun Head, also in County Wexford, and at both locations the signal mast was erected close to but not on the tower itself.

The original estimated cost for each south-coast tower was to have been £2,000, but the actual figure eventually averaged well over £3,000 and the cost of some of the larger east-coast towers rose to almost £7,000. The final total for the line of 103 was therefore somewhere in the region of £350,000, an enormous sum at that time to be spent on fixed defences. The Irish towers were somewhat cheaper to build, averaging between £2-3,000 each; this probably reflected the lower cost of labour in Ireland and the fact that the towers were built of stone rather than brick. Total expenditure on the Irish towers came to a further £150-175,000, and these figures are an interesting insight into the amount of money available to the Board of Ordnance in a time of national emergency and over which Parliament appears to have had little control. There was little criticism of this expenditure at the time, understandably with Napoleon poised to invade. Criticism of these defences and the amount of money spent on them came later. In 1823 William Cobbett denounced the construction of the towers as a total waste of money when he visited Kent, but, like many critics of military expenditure throughout history, his criticism came with the benefit of hindsight and after the money had been spent.

Martello towers were also built in Scotland and the Orkneys and were similar in design to the English versions; but in the Channel Islands there are gun towers sometimes referred to as 'Martello towers' which were built earlier than the south-coast towers, were smaller and of quite a different design. These are frequently referred to as 'pre-Martello towers', but they are still a part of this story since their construction late in the eighteenth century undoubtedly had an influence on the construction of the Martello towers proper twenty years later.

Some other large gun towers were built much later in the nineteenth century, between 1840 and 1860, and, although often referred to as Martello towers, did not follow the earlier designs. Towers built at Pembroke Dock in Wales to defend the dockyard are known locally as the North East and the South West Martello Tower, and the notice requesting tenders for the building of a tower on Stack Rock in Milford Haven indicated that the tender was for the construction of a 'Martello tower'. Two further large towers were built, one on the Spit of Grain opposite Sheerness in Kent and the second on the Brehon Rock off Guernsey. All these, with the exception of the South West Martello Tower at Pembroke Dock, were oval in shape and mounted two or three guns.

CHAPTER 2

The English South and East Coast Defences

The line of 103 Martello towers in Sussex, Kent, Essex and Suffolk was designed to meet the specific threat of French invasion. The Peace of Amiens in 1802 brought only a temporary respite in the long war with revolutionary France. After fourteen months of uneasy peace, the British government, feeling threatened by the continued French expansionist foreign policy and in particular by Napoleon's control of Holland, declared war on France on 18 May 1803. Napoleon regarded Britain as his most dangerous enemy and between 1803 and 1805 all French military resources were devoted to planning and executing the invasion of England. An army of 160,000 troops in six corps was assembled in the Pas de Calais area and enormous efforts were made to assemble enough shipping and barges to convey the army across the Channel.

The total strength of the British Army in England, including the Militia, was about 130,000, and quite clearly this total was insufficient to protect the complete length of the coastline from invasion, even with the addition of the numerous but poorly armed and poorly trained Volunteers. The Commander-in-Chief, the Duke of York, in a report dated 25 August 1803, made it clear that the priority must be the defence of London and the major naval ports.[1] By a process of elimination based on geographical factors, the threatened areas of the east coast were reduced to Hollesley Bay, the beach between the Deben and the Orwell, Harwich and Clacton Beach. The south coast,

Photograph of about 1870, looking from Langney Redoubt to the line of towers (66-61) in Pevensey Bay, Sussex. [East Sussex County Library]

however, was considered to be more vulnerable to invasion since the distance from the invasion ports to the English beaches was so much shorter. Here the threatened areas were defined as the beaches from Folkestone to Dymchurch in Kent, the area from Rye to the start of the cliffs just east of Hastings, and Pevensey Bay from Bulverhythe to Eastbourne in Sussex. In the Commander-in-Chief's plan more than half the available troops were to be allocated to the Southern and the Eastern District, the two military districts most obviously threatened with invasion, and 50,000 men were to be stationed in Kent and Sussex - the Southern District - to prevent an enemy advance on London.

This report was not the first to consider in detail how the English coastline should be defended against the French. An earlier one in April 1798, made by Major Thomas Reynolds of the 30th Foot as a result of his inspection of the defences of the south and the east coast, was the first to put forward a proposal for a line of towers to supplement the existing defences. On completion of his inspection he recommended the building of a line of ninety-eight towers between Littlestone in Sussex and Yarmouth in Norfolk and in support of his proposal Reynolds quoted the success of the tower at Mortella Point in beating off the two British ships, together with the views of Marshal Saxe on the use of towers as land defences.[2] Reynolds's suggested towers resembled the towers built earlier on Jersey rather than the later Martello towers, having thinner walls and a line of twelve loopholes in the wall. Interestingly, although not an engineer officer, he calculated that each tower would require 300,000 bricks and cost in the region of £2,000, figures remarkably similar to those calculated some years later for the actual Martello towers.

Reynolds's plan did not find favour at the time, not least because the total cost would have been so enormous and public opinion lacked the spur of imminent invasion. But five years later, in July 1803, the situation was very different when Captain W.H. Ford, a Royal Engineers officer stationed at Dover, proposed the building of a line of square towers along the threatened coasts, each to be two storeys in height, surmounted by a platform carrying a heavy gun. He submitted his proposal to Brigadier-General William Twiss, the Commanding Engineer Southern District, and he forwarded the proposal to General Dundas, commanding Southern District, but recommended that the towers should be built adjacent to existing batteries. Dundas had served in Corsica and was aware of the defensive potential of properly sited gun towers and he, in turn, endorsed the proposal although he thought the construction of the towers would take time and would not produce an immediate defence of the coast.

Because of the delay in dealing with business which resulted from the huge workload imposed on the Board of Ordnance the proposal for the line of towers might have ended there had the matter of the defence of the south coast not become a political one. In April 1804 the Committee of Engineers, which advised the Board of Ordnance, was summoned to report to the Cabinet on the proposal and stated that the Committee could not recommend towers as having any advantage over a battery with the same number of guns. With the Admiralty strongly supporting the construction of towers and at least one Member of Parliament raising the matter in the Commons the Board proposed a revised scheme using circular towers to supplement existing or proposed batteries at thirteen sites along the Kent and the Sussex coast for a total cost of £57,000.[3] Brigadier-General Twiss was instructed to survey suitable locations and to be responsible for the construction of the towers.

By September 1804 this limited scheme was in abeyance and Twiss, on instructions from Pitt, once again the Prime Minister, and Colonel Hope, Deputy Quartermaster-General, was ordered to reactivate the plan for eighty-eight towers, now at an estimated cost of £221,000.[4] The fear of invasion in the minds of the public was by now approaching panic proportions and the Privy Council felt it necessary to call a meeting at Rochester on 21 October 1804 to consider the whole matter of the defences of southern England. The meeting was attended by the Duke of York, Pitt, his brother the Earl of Chatham (then Master General of the Ordnance), General Dundas, General Brownrigg (Quartermaster- General), Major-General Morse (Inspector General of Fortifications) and Twiss, together with a number of other officers.

Plan and section of a round tower, possibly the designed submitted to the Rochester Conference in 1804. [PRO WO 55/778]

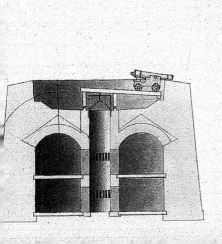
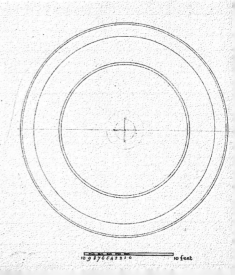

When considering the problem of defence against invasion the meeting had the benefit of two detailed studies. In addition to the report signed by the Commander-in-Chief the previous year, there was a second study of the English defences written by a renegade French general Dumourriez between his arrival in England in 1803 and May 1804. Victor of Valmy and Jemappes but disillusioned with the new government of the Republic after the execution of the king, Dumourriez fled France in 1793 after an abortive attempt to lead the army against the regicides. After wandering the continent he arrived in England and, through his friendship with Lord Nelson and other prominent men, was accepted as a military adviser by the government. His report covered all aspects of the defence of England against invasion and, most importantly, confirmed that the areas already identified by the Commander-in-Chief were, indeed, those where the French were most likely to land.[5]

At this meeting Pitt and members of the Board of Ordnance pushed through the proposal for the larger number of towers. The only dissenting voice was that of Lieutenant-Colonel Brown, RE, who had recently proposed the building of a canal to run from Hythe to Rye, where it was to join the Rother Navigation. Brown was bitterly opposed to the idea of a line of towers and in his diary on 21 October 1804 he wrote:

> 'The expensive and diabolical system of Tower Defence was finally resolved on to an unprecedented extent, contrary to the opinions of the best and most experienced officers in our service; but it was caused by the influence of the Ordnance people only - whose opinions were by no means supported by reasoning. Mr Pitt, from whom one would have expected a decided opinion, gave in to that of others and without requiring, what indeed he would not have obtained, a satisfactory and well-digested plan of defence, all that was advanced was Tower, Tower, Tower; some large and some small was all the variation proposed by the engineers, and when General Morse was asked if he thought even the number of towers proposed would be sufficient, he thought not, but proposed to place cannon in open batteries between them.'[6]

The Rochester conference originally proposed that the line of towers should consist of eighty-six circular ones of three types: a large tower mounting eleven guns, a smaller tower mounting four and the smallest with a single gun.[7] Six weeks after the conference, on 3 December, Brigadier-General Twiss wrote to the Earl of Chatham:

> 'I certainly approve of a Tower for Eleven Guns instead of one for Four,

at the Places mentioned at Rochester viz: at the Sea Houses, and the Entrance to Rye Harbour in Sussex, and at the East End of Dymchurch Wall in Kent. I still think that a Tower for Four Guns is well calculated for Anthony Hill, at least I know of no other work that appears to me so appropriate to this situation.' [8]

Further consideration of the sites for the structures reduced the number of small towers to seventy-four, including the tower of Sandgate Castle, one of Henry VIII's 'Great Castles', which was to be reconstructed and strengthened. The tower of the castle was provided with a bomb-proof roof supported by a central pillar, as in the Martello towers, and armed with a single 24pdr gun on a traversing platform.

The proposal that three large towers and one for four guns should be built was also reduced to two large towers for eleven guns each. These towers, which were really circular redoubts, were to be built as planned at Eastbourne (Sea Houses) in Sussex and at Dymchurch in Kent, but the idea of defending Rye Harbour and Anthony Hill with larger towers was dropped and the decision was taken instead to build a small tower surrounded by a ditch at each location. The large towers or redoubts each mounted eleven 24pdr guns and were surrounded by a ditch 25ft (7.6m) wide and the ditch of the Eastbourne redoubt was defended by five small caponiers. Each redoubt was garrisoned by eight officers and 320 soldiers. Together with these redoubts and towers, two further fortifications were built to protect the south coast at Dover, the Citadel and the Drop Redoubt on the Western Heights. Construction of the larger of these, the Citadel, was stopped in 1815 and it was not until 1853 that work to complete it was resumed.

Model of the Eastbourne Redoubt; this mounted eleven guns although only ten are shown on the model. [Eastbourne Redoubt Museum]

Lieutenant-Colonel Brown's opposition to the towers was unavailing and once the decision to build them had been taken it remained only to overcome the numerous building problems presented by such a large scheme of fortification. The Committee of Engineers recommended building with bricks and Brigadier-General Twiss calculated that each tower would require almost a quarter of a million, a total of more than 20 million if the eighty-six towers originally proposed were built.[9] The Inspector General of Fortifications, Major-General Morse, authorized the purchase of bricks from Adam and Robertson, a London firm of builders' merchants, even before the Board of Ordnance had confirmed the contract. In turn, Adam and Robertson subcontracted the order to eleven brick works around London and the south-east of England in order to prevent speculation and to keep the price of bricks from escalating.[10] The number of bricks ordered in 1804 for the towers came to a total of 13.45 million at a total cost to the Board of Ordnance of £37,450.[11] In 1805 William Hobson, a Quaker, was appointed the main contractor for both the south and the east coast towers, but the actual construction was frequently subcontacted leading to varying standards of workmanship. Two of the main subcontractors, Edward Hodges and John Smith, together with William Hobson are said to have made their fortunes thereby.

A problem presented to the defenders of Kent had always been what to do with the Dungeness peninsula and the area of Romney Marsh. Although both were considered to be vulnerable to an enemy landing, Dungeness was considered to be less of a problem because of the difficulty of moving guns and wagons over the deep shingle. Even before the Treaty of Amiens in 1801 the plan had been to leave the defence of the peninsula to a redoubt and four batteries at Dungeness itself - together known as the Dungeness Bastion - and so the plan for a line of Martello towers did not cover this area. For the defence of Romney Marsh there was an existing plan which involved the flooding of the marsh, but this was unpopular with the local inhabitants and considered to be militarily impracticable since it would take as long as three days before the water would be deep enough to form an impassable barrier.

In 1804, before the Rochester conference, Lieutenant-Colonel Brown had suggested adding a canal to the proposed defences of the coast to act as a wet ditch. This was to run from Shorncliffe, near Hythe in Kent, to Hastings, cutting off the base of the Dungeness peninsula. The Royal Military Canal, as it was named, was built by John Rennie, the leading canal expert of the day, and eventually ran for almost 26 miles (42km). The canal, together with a military road running alongside it, was completed in 1809. This was used not only as a defensive ditch, with batteries at each bend, but also for navigation, providing, together with the road, a greatly improved transport system for the area. Tower 30, which still remains today, was sited almost two miles inland on the Rye to Winchelsea road in order to protect the Royal Military Canal sluices, while six other towers were sited to protect the Romney Marsh sluices nearer the sea. The six towers, Nos.22 to 27, were sited in pairs to protect the Willop, Marshland and Globsden Glut sluices and Towers 24 and 25, which protected the main Marshland sluice at Dymchurch, both still exist.

In 1805 a plan for a further fifty-five towers, two circular batteries and a redoubt to defend the east coast between Brightlingsea in Essex and Aldeburgh in Suffolk was put forward. This was subsequently reduced, probably on the grounds of economy, to twenty-eight small towers, one large one and a redoubt at Harwich. The east-coast towers, as we have seen, were larger than the towers on the south coast, but the Harwich redoubt was similar to those at Eastbourne and Dymchurch, but mounted only ten guns. The two circular batteries, included in the original plan, were to have protected the entrance to Orford Haven and the beach at Aldeburgh, and were noted in an estimate for bricks dated 27 June 1806 as requiring 600,000 each.[12] Neither of these batteries was built and, instead,

Tower CC at Aldeburgh, Suffolk; this unusual tower was the only one of its type to be built. [Author's photograph]

Tower BB was erected on a shingle bank near the mouth of the River Ore, only to be demolished in 1822 when it became unsafe, and the large tower, Tower CC, was built on Aldeburgh beach.

Tower CC was unique since it was quatrefoil in shape and mounted four 24pdr guns. Unlike the standard towers it had no central pillar and the roof was supported by a vaulted arch. It was built to a design which, it has since been suggested, was originally planned for a tower to be situated at the end of the Dymchurch wall in Kent where the Dymchurch Redoubt now stands. This seems unlikely and it is more probable that the design of Tower CC took into account that it would stand alone on a shingle bank with water in front and behind and where it was necessary to cover the approaches from all points of the compass. The Aldeburgh tower stood alone almost 10 miles (16 km) north of Tower BB because the area between them was not considered to be vulnerable to an enemy landing since the Rivers Ore and Alde formed a barrier immediately behind the beach.

Aldeburgh was also protected by an existing open battery of four guns and, indeed, the majority of the east coast towers were built in conjunction with batteries. In this way they differed from the south-coast models where only Towers 66 and 74 had a battery adjacent to them. On the east coast only Towers H, O, P, S, U, Z and BB stood alone while the remainder were sited alongside batteries most of which were armed with three 24pdr guns, although ten batteries were larger with between four and seven guns each.

Finally, there was the need to find sufficient trained soldiers to garrison the line of towers and to man the batteries of the Royal Military Canal. By 1804 all troops were already committed to the existing defence plans but it was estimated that the towers along the south and the east coast needed a minimum of a further 3,000 troops. A number of proposals were put forward, including the formation of a Corps of Coast Fencibles and the formation of a second battalion for each of the Royal Artillery battalions to act as depot and training units as with the Line battalions of infantry. The Earl of Chatham did not support this latter proposal and, since the only readily available sources of manpower were the Veteran and Invalid battalions and the newly formed Volunteers, it is not surprising that we find him writing to Castlereagh in 1805: 'I incline strongly to the opinion that the best garrison for the Towers will be the Veteran Battalions assisted occasionally by Volunteer Corps of Artillery many of which are very good...a portion of the Invalid Battalion [of Artillery] would of course be attached for the service of the Towers.'[13]

CHAPTER 3

CHAPTER 3

The Fate of the English Towers

1805-1960

Of the seventy-four towers built in Kent and Sussex only twenty-six still stand today and these are in varying condition. Ten have been converted at some time or other into private residences or holiday homes while four others, Towers 3, 24, 73 and 74, are open to the public. One, Tower 66 at Langney Point near Eastbourne, was used until recently by HM Coastguard, and the remainder, including Towers 6, 7, and 9, which are still owned by the Ministry of Defence, are unoccupied and derelict. The majority of the south-coast towers have, however, simply vanished. A few fell to developers or local authority planners, but for the rest the enemy was Nature itself and, positioned as they were on the shingle shore, they simply fell into the sea.

The dismantling and disarming of the towers started as early as 1818, although Tower 29 at Rye Harbour was abandoned as early as 1809 because of the danger from the sea; it was subsequently demolished in 1822, together with Tower 45 near Bulverhythe. The materials from both of these were sold to a local company, Breeds and Company, realising £220 for Tower 29 and £349 for 45.[1] On the east coast a number of towers were sold in 1819, but those in Kent and Sussex were considered still to be an important element of the coastal fortifications and it was some years before the effects of coastal erosion caused a number to be disposed of. In 1873 a report on coast defences showed that fifty-eight of the towers in Kent and Sussex remained, though some were in poor or even dangerous condition. Eight were shown as 'disarmed' and eight of the missing sixteen, Towers 44 to 51 along the coast past Bexhill, were noted as having disappeared through coastal erosion.[2]

By 1817 all the guns on the towers in the Hythe Division, Nos. 1 to 27 in Kent, had been removed with their carriages and traversing platforms to the Ordnance store at Shorncliffe Camp, and two years later it was reported that the guns had also been removed from Towers 52 to 73 in Sussex.[3] The towers were still maintained and in some cases groins were proposed and sometimes built to slow the pace of erosion by the sea. As early as 1811 the foundations of Tower 54 at Cooden in Pevensey Bay were exposed by high winds and tides, and

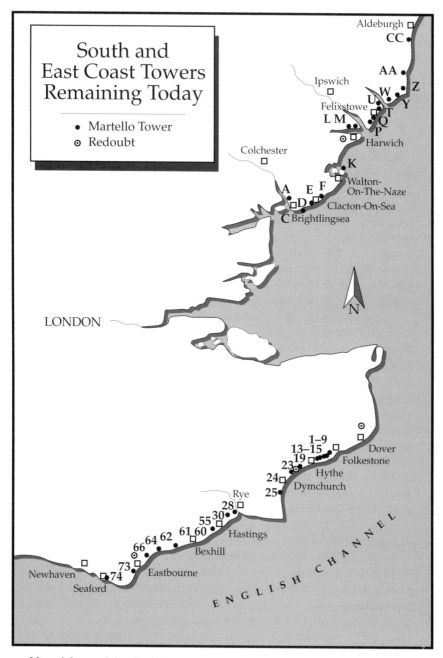

Map of the surviving English towers. [Michael Pugh]

in a letter from Captain Goffsett, RE to Major Handfield, RE there is an intriguing insight into military-civilian relations at that time. Goffsett wrote:

> '*I suspect that the Commissioners of Pevensey Level when they placed the groin to the West of our Tower believed it would endanger it so much as to induce Government to put one to the Eastward; where I conceive they must place one for the security of their land if Government does not do it. But by our mode of proceeding, I think we shall jocky them, and oblige them to do what they so kindly intended we should.*'[4]

The phrase 'our mode of proceeding' was obviously an ironical reference to the length of time it took to obtain a decision from the Board of Ordnance. Who built the additional groin for the defence of the tower against erosion is not certain, but in 1873 the condition of the tower was described as 'precarious' and by the beginning of this century it had disappeared together with Towers 52 and 53.

The construction of the towers had an unexpected effect on a major problem facing the civil authorities at that time. Smuggling had been prevalent along the Kent and the Sussex coast since 1700, with the smugglers operating successfully and profitably despite all the efforts of the Customs officers and the officers of the Excise to stop them. The construction of the Martello towers and, in particular, the Royal Military Canal, which cut off Romney Marsh and prevented the smugglers from using this route to land their contraband, reduced smuggling considerably until the end of the Napoleonic War in 1815.

Tower 24 at Dymchurch, Kent in the early 1900s when it was used as a Coastguard station; the exterior brick staircase was added to each remaining tower at the end of the nineteenth century. [Author's collection]

With its end smuggling again became a serious problem for the authorities and in 1817-18 the Coast Blockade was established, using naval officers and sailors based in Martello towers or watch houses to prevent smugglers from landing their cargoes along the most vulnerable stretches of the south coast. Among the towers and other fortifications used by the Blockade and the Coastguard, which succeeded it in 1831, were Towers 1, 3, 4, 22, 23, 24, 26 and 27 along the Kent coast, a tower at Bexhill and Towers 73 and 74 in Sussex.

Later in the century a limited attempt was made to modernize the armament of some of the towers. Of those which received more modern guns seven were equipped with a single 68pdr gun in place of the original 24pdr and fourteen had 32pdr guns. Tower 30 at Rye was rearmed with one 7in 110pdr Armstrong BL gun on a dwarf traversing platform - a platform with shortened legs which reduced the height the gun stood above the parapet and was most usually employed when a gun was mounted firing through an embrasure.

On the east coast, where all but five of the remaining nineteen towers had been disarmed, Towers L, M, N, P and Q around Harwich, Felixstowe and the mouths of the Stour and Orwell rivers were each armed with one 68pdr and two 8in shell guns. By 1887 Tower N was still in use as part of the defences of Harwich, guarding the northern bank of the Orwell. At that date this interesting tower had, in addition to its own armament of three guns, a new battery for three 9in 12-ton RML guns, built in 1872 on the site of the original four-gun battery. This battery was mounted on the glacis on the river side of the tower's ditch, but forming an integrated defensive position with the tower. The approach to the tower and the battery was through a new gateway built in 1871 on the landward side of the ditch, up a long, sloping ramp set on iron piers which crossed the ditch and cunette. The ramp ended in a drawbridge which was raised and lowered by a winch within the tower.[5] Together with Landguard Fort and the fourteen-gun battery on Shotley peninsula, Tower N became an important constituent of the defences of Harwich in the late nineteenth century.

A number of towers were deliberately destroyed by the War Office. The period from 1860 to 1875 was one great advances in the design of artillery and the development of explosives, and a number of armies, including the British Army, wished to experiment in order to discover exactly how effective the new rifled guns were when used against masonry fortifications. In 1860 the War Department used Towers 49 and 71 for a comparative study of the effects of both the old and the new guns when firing against a masonry structure and in the same year the Prussian Army carried out a similar experiment against the small fortress of Juliers. Smooth-bore 32pdr and 68pdr guns were used against Tower 49 while against Tower 71 three guns were used, a rifled 80pdr, a rifled 40pdr and a 7in howitzer. A major breach was opened in Tower 71 after forty-seven rounds of a mixture of solid shot and live shell had been fired, and after a further 158 rounds had been despatched the rear wall of the tower had completely collapsed. However, the smooth-bore guns were unable to make any serious impression on Tower 49 with a similar number of rounds.[6]

There is some dispute concerning the number of towers actually used in the artillery trials. Sheila Sutcliffe in her book includes Towers 50 and 68 together with 71 as those destroyed in the trials but makes no mention of Tower 49.[7] However, the *Royal Engineers Journal* in 1874 describes the result of the trials using Towers 49 and 71 but, in its turn, makes no mention of the other two, and the Report on Coast Defences of 1873 states that Tower 50 had disappeared by 1856 and showed that Tower 68 still existed when the report was compiled.[8] A further artillery trial was carried out in 1876 when guns firing from Anthony Hill and the glacis of the Eastbourne redoubt engaged specially constructed concrete casemates between Towers 65 and 66 together with the remains of Tower 70 which had already collapsed as a result of coastal erosion. A photograph of the gun position used in the trial is of interest as it shows in the background the top of Tower 68 with a Union flag flying from the flagpole.

The first artillery trials were followed in 1872-74 by the destruction of Towers 10, 26, 35 and 38 in a further study, this time concerning the explosive effect of the new gun cotton when compared with gunpowder. Tower 10, situated below Shorncliffe Camp on the outskirts of Hythe required 200lb (90kg) of gun cotton before it was finally destroyed, while slightly less, 196lb (88kg) was needed to produce the same result at Tower 26. Towers 35 and 38 were demolished by using a similar quantity of gun cotton together with 800lb (363kg) of gunpowder.[9]

Towards the end of the nineteenth century the pace of destruction continued, although more slowly. In addition to the removal of Tower 10, both Nos.11 and 12 were also demolished to permit the building of the promenade along the seafront at Hythe, probably between 1872 and 1880. Tower 59 was demolished in 1903 to make way for an estate of houses, a precedent set by the demolition of Tower 68, also demolished to enable houses to be built some years earlier. Towers 16, 17, 18 and 65 had collapsed into the sea by 1938 and it is thought that by 1940 Tower 63 had been either demolished by a developer or by the Royal Engineers. Certainly its demolition is something of a

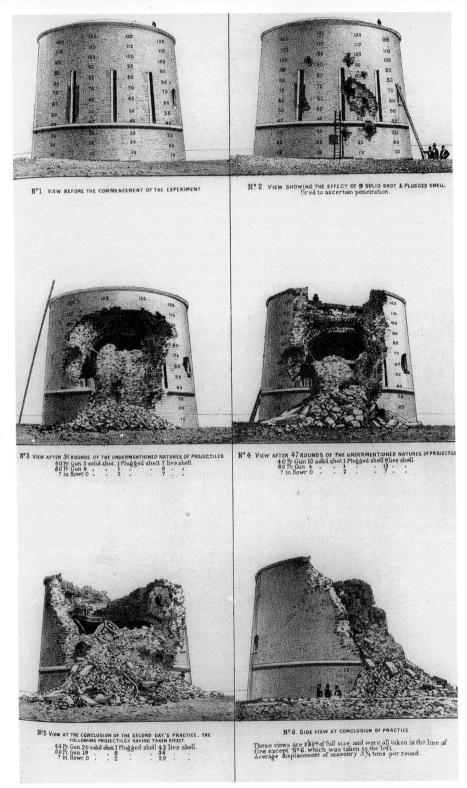

Nº1. VIEW BEFORE THE COMMENCEMENT OF THE EXPERIMENT.

Nº2. VIEW SHOWING THE EFFECT OF 9 SOLID SHOT & PLUGGED SHELL,
fired to ascertain penetration.

Nº3. VIEW AFTER 31 ROUNDS OF THE UNDERMENTIONED NATURES OF PROJECTILES.
40 Pr Gun 3 solid shot 1 Plugged shell 7 live shell.
80 Pr Gun 4 " 1 " 6 "
7 in Howr 0 " 2 " 7 "

Nº4. VIEW AFTER 47 ROUNDS OF THE UNDERMENTIONED NATURES OF PROJECTILES
40 Pr Gun 10 solid shot 1 Plugged shell 9 live shell.
80 Pr Gun 4 " 1 " 13 "
7 in Howr 0 " 2 " 7 "

Nº5 VIEW AT THE CONCLUSION OF THE SECOND DAY'S PRACTICE. THE
FOLLOWING PROJECTILES HAVING TAKEN EFFECT.
40 Pr Gun 20 solid shot 1 Plugged shell 43 live shell.
80 Pr Gun 19 " 8 " 36 "
7 in Howr 0 " 2 " 29 "

Nº6. SIDE VIEW AT CONCLUSION OF PRACTICE.
These views are 2⅝% of full size, and were all taken in the line of
fire except Nº6, which was taken to the left.
Average displacement of masonry 3½ tons per round.

*Tower 71 in Pevensey Bay, near Eastbourne, was used as a target in the artillery
trials in 1860; the picture shows the progressive damage from rifled guns.* [PRO WO
33/9]

mystery since it was standing in the late 1920s but by 1945 had disappeared and local legend has it that the bricks and rubble were used to build a local RAF airfield. The last tower on the the south coast to disappear, Tower 22, was demolished by Kent County Council in 1956 in order to widen the road at Dymchurch where the tower, built between the sea wall and the road, was considered to be an obstruction.

In 1940 the towers were once again taken into use for the very reason for which they were first designed, namely defence against invasion. Those closest to the beaches, particularly those along the Sussex coast between Bexhill and Eastbourne, had concrete observation and command posts built on their gun platforms, and among the towers adapted in this manner were Towers 55, 64, 66 and 73. Those towers actually standing on the beach became strongpoints and had their windows converted into concrete loopholes for light machine-guns and additional firing positions for heavy machine-guns were opened in the tower wall close to the ground. Tower 73, the Wish Tower, at Eastbourne had a fire-control post built on its top to control the fire of two 6in BL coastal defence guns sited in concrete emplacements close to the tower. In late 1940 and early 1941, when the invasion threat was at its greatest, the towers were manned by regular troops, and Tower 24 at Dymchurch was manned for a time by a Forward Observation party from 64 Field Regiment RA based in the Dymchurch and New Romney area, while 552 Coast Defence Regiment RA manned the Wish Tower. Later, as the threat dimin-

Tower 64 at Pevensey Bay, sited on the flat shingle beach; the tower was used in 1940 as an observation post and for beach defence; additional concrete protection was added to the gun platform and the windows were converted into loopholes. [Author's photograph]

ished, the towers were taken over by local Home Guard units.

In Essex and Suffolk sixteen of the towers had been disarmed by 1818; two were used by the Coast Blockade and one, Tower O, had been converted into a powder magazine. Four towers, G, H, I and V, were sold and demolished for building materials as early as 1819 or 1820, and a fifth tower, BB, was sold in 1822 when it became apparent that the shingle bank on which it was built would not support it without considerable expense to reinforce its foundations. Tower R was demolished early in this century and Tower B was taken down to make way for a housing estate in 1967. Tower N, which had been in military use until the end of the nineteenth century, was in ruins by 1948 and was finally built over when the new Felixstowe container port was constructed in the 1980s.

The Towers Today

Although only twenty-six out of seventy-four south-coast towers remain, on the east coast it is still possible to see eighteen of the original twenty-nine. Of these forty-four towers, ten are currently privately occupied as either permanent residences or holiday homes of which seven, Towers 1, 2, 8, 13, 23, 60 and 62, are in Kent and Sussex, and three, Q, W and AA in Suffolk. Tower 13 has been a private house longer than any of the others, having been disposed of by the War Department in 1906. It was bought for use as a house in 1928 but it was not until after the Second World War, during which it was used as an artillery command post, that it was purchased by Ronald Ward, FRIBA and, in 1960, rather unsympathetically converted. These words are used because Mr Ward overcame the the problem of a lack of internal light by opening a number of large windows in the section of the wall facing the sea. It was a major work to enlarge the windows and it is an indication of the problem and of the strength of the Martello towers that it took two men with a compressor and two guns three weeks to make a cavity in the wall 7 x 7 x 3 cu.ft (2.1 x 2.1 x 0.9 cu. m) for a wardrobe.[10]

Tower Q, on South Hill in Felixstowe, was given up by the War Department in 1946 and has been a private residence since then. It too has been the subject of an unsympathetic conversion and has had an unnecessary crenellation added to the parapet which detracts from the usual simplicity of the tower's outline. A driveway has been opened from the street through the counterscarp of the ditch and the ditch itself has been made into a garden.

Tower 13 on the West Parade at Hythe, Kent; this was converted into a house in 1960 with little consideration for its historic design or the attractiveness of its appearance. [Author's photograph]

The eight other towers are more recent remodellings. On the whole, the work has been carried out with greater consideration for the historic integrity of each tower. Towers 23, W and AA have retained their original appearance almost without alteration, while Towers 8, 60 and 62 have had sun rooms built on their gun platforms. Tower 8, at the top of Hospital Hill at Shorncliffe near Folkestone, is probably the best of the more recent conversions and has managed to retain its original character, including the ditch which is now a garden. A bridge has been used to approach the door and the sun room on top has been provided with a low, conical, slate roof rather than a flat one as in the other conversions, and the chimney has been retained, though raised somewhat in height.

Tower CC at Aldeburgh in Suffolk was offered for sale in 1932

Tower 8 at Shorncliffe, near Folkestone; this is a good example of a sympathetic conversion into a permanent dwelling. [Author's photograph]

through William Whiteley Ltd, the London firm of auctioneers, having been previously used as an Admiralty signal station. Situated about a mile south of the town, the tower is actually the only surviving building of the little village of Slaughden and was purchased for use as a residence. The new owner commissioned the architect Justin Vulliamy to convert it into a house which he did by building a concrete superstructure on the gun platform. During the Second World War the Army occupied the tower and afterwards it was left derelict. In 1971 the tower was taken over by the Landmark Trust which removed the superstructure, renovated the interior and it is now available for holiday lettings.[11]

A number of other towers have previously been used as dwellings but are now no longer occupied. Tower 30, which stands today surrounded by a scrap yard on the Winchelsea Road on the outskirts of Rye, was once occupied but is now derelict. Tower 55, at Norman's Bay near Pevensey, is in rather better condition and has recently been offered for sale with a view to reconversion to a house. Before the Second World War this tower was used as a summer residence and earlier still, in 1905, had been used by Mr A.T.M. Johnson for exper-

iments in wireless telegraphy. Another tower which had previously
been occupied is No.61, but this is now the centrepiece of the
Martello housing estate near Pevensey and still retains on its gun platform the two-storey, concrete, position-finding post constructed
during the Second World War. It too is no longer occupied.

Two towers, Tower 66 at Langney Point near Eastbourne and Tower
P on Fort Road at Felixstowe, were used until quite recently by HM
Coastguard. Tower P has been purchased by Suffolk Coastal District
Council and it remains to be seen what use it will make of it. Tower
F, at Clacton-on-Sea, was also used by the Coastguard and more
recently by the Sea Scouts. All three towers remain in reasonable
condition.

Four towers on the south coast and one on the east coast are open
to the public. On the Warren at Folkestone, Tower 3 has been
converted into a tourist information centre by the town council and
still retains its Second World War observation post on the gun platform. Tower 24, at Dymchurch, also in Kent, was acquired from the
War Department by the Ministry of Works in 1959 when it was no
longer required by the Coastguard. It was restored to its original state
and was opened to visitors in 1969; today it is in the care of English
Heritage and open to visitors at weekends during the summer months.
Tower 73, after a long period as a tea room, has now been reopened
as a puppet and toy museum, but the tower may still be inspected,
and Tower 74, at Seaford, has also been restored and is in use as a
museum of local history. On the east coast Tower A, at St. Osyth near
Brightlingsea, is now the home of the East Essex Aviation Museum.

To complete the story of the south and the east coast defences it is
perhaps worth mentioning the fate of the three redoubts which were
an integral part of the line of towers. All three remain today and the
Eastbourne and the Harwich Redoubt are in the hands of local trusts
which maintain them and open both to the public. The Eastbourne
Redoubt, in addition, houses the Sussex Combined Services Museum
and the regimental museum of a cavalry regiment. The Dymchurch
Redoubt remains under the control of the Ministry of Defence
(Army) and is part of the complex of live firing ranges at Hythe.

CHAPTER 4

The Spanish and the Minorcan Towers

Defensive towers had been in use along the Mediterranean littoral for centuries to protect harbours, anchorages and small towns, and to give warning of raids, particularly by corsairs. The tower at Mortella Point was one example of a common type and the remains of others may still be seen on Corsica and along the Spanish and the Italian coast. In the middle of the eighteenth century the Spanish built five towers on the Canary Islands with the role of defending them from pirates and enemies such as the British, while on Minorca they built two similar towers some thirty years later in 1780-81.

Two of the five existing towers on the Canary Islands were built on the island of Gran Canaria and one, the Castillo de San Cristobel, was one of the earliest to be built. This tower, constructed to defend the shoreline on the southern outskirts of the capital Las Palmas, was built by Don Diego de Melgarejo in 1577, but today is in ruinous condition. The second tower, the Torre de Gando, was situated further south in the Bay of Gando. It was completed in 1741 on the foundations of

The refurbished tower at Gando on the island of Gran Canaria. [Author's collection]

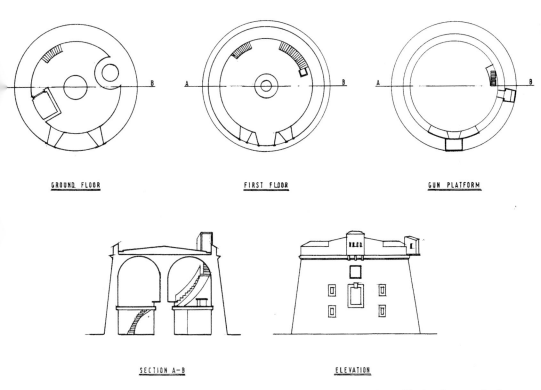

GROUND FLOOR   FIRST FLOOR   GUN PLATFORM

SECTION A–B   ELEVATION

Section and plan of the Gando tower; a comparison of its outline with the photograph shows that when the tower was reconstructed in 1980 the parapet was not rebuilt to the original height. [Greg Cox]

an earlier sixteenth-century tower and is today within the perimeter of the Spanish Air Force base at Gando Airport. The Gando tower demonstrates all the basic design features that were to be used in the later English Martello towers. It was 27ft (8.4m) high with a diameter at the base of 35ft (10.75m) and at the parapet of 31ft (9.6m). Access was by means of a removable ladder and inside the tower the basement and the gun platform were reached by means of a wooden staircase built close to the inner wall. There was a central pillar supporting an arched roof and the gun platform, on which were mounted three 12pdr guns. Projecting from the parapet of the platform there was a machicolation over the doorway and a small latrine. The basement contained a cistern and storeroom and the whole tower was built of rubble masonry.[1] The Gando tower was repaired and refurbished in 1980, but access is restricted as it stands within a military zone.

Of the other three towers in the Canary Islands one was built on Lanzarote, at Las Coloredas near Playa Blanca, and two on Fuerteventura, at Caleta de Fustes south of Puerto del Rosario and on the coast near the village of Rocque in the north-west of the island. The tower at Caleta de Fustes is larger than the Gran Canaria towers with gun embrasures in the parapet wall, but in other respects it conforms to the same design. The tower is now part of an hotel and holiday complex and appears to be in good condition.

Minorca, on which the Spanish subsequently built two more towers, was ceded, together with Gibraltar, to Britain by Spain under the Treaty of Utrecht in 1713. Minorca remained a British possesion for over sixty years, with only a brief interruption between 1756 and 1763 when the French occupied the island, until it was lost to Spain in 1782 during the American War of Independence. The British recovered the island from the Spanish in 1798 but held it only until 1802, but in that time it again became the principal Royal Navy base in the Mediterranean. The Canary Islands towers and the two on Minorca would have been known to many Navy and Marine officers (Nelson himself lost his arm in an attack on Tenerife in the Canary Islands) and it may be concluded that these towers served as the principal models when the British engineers came to build eleven more on Minorca. Indeed, it is probably correct to say that although it was the

Map of Minorca. [Michael Pugh]

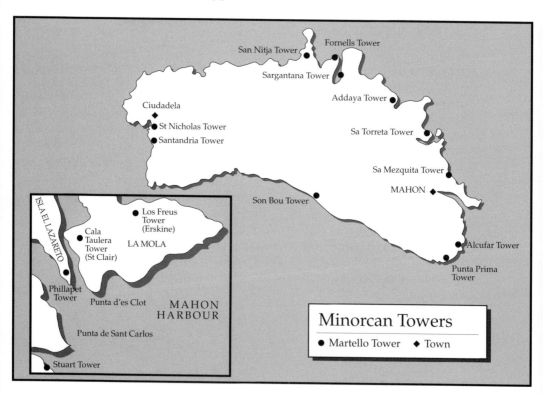

success of the tower at Mortella Point in repulsing the Royal Navy ships which brought gun towers into favour as a relatively cheap form of coastal defence, it was actually the towers in the Canary Islands and on Minorca that were to be the prototypes of all the later Martello towers.

The commander of the expedition to capture Minorca and its first governor after the island's reoccupation was Lieutenant-General Sir Charles Stuart, an experienced soldier who had no illusions regarding the difficulties inherent in defending it. Stuart appreciated that it would be almost impossible to defend the main port of Mahon without building major fortifications which would require a much larger garrison than he had at his disposal. In a letter dated 2 March 1799 Stuart wrote: 'The Navy should Ever be the principal Bulwark of the Island.'[2] He had already advised the government in London that he meant to hold the island by opposing the enemy at their point of landing while using a mobile reserve of troops to destroy any who managed to advance clear of the defended beaches. To this end General Stuart ordered the immediate construction of seven towers which were 'Calculated more for the temporary protection of different places' and were to be 'Combined with a further plan of encountering the Enemy wherever they may effect a descent.'[3]

Of the first seven towers to be built four were to defend the immediate approaches to Mahon from the sea. A fifth and two batteries were built at Sa Mesquita, a beach to the north east of Mahon where a successful landing by an enemy force would outflank the defences of La Mola, a projecting headland which dominated the entrance to the harbour and the narrow channel leading to Mahon, and the Phillipet peninsula close to it. The sixth tower, known as Sa Torreta (or Torre Rambla) defended a beach and anchorage north of Sa Mesquita, while the seventh was built on the other side of the island to defend the old capital of Ciudadela. Here the British also partially rebuilt the seventeenth-century, octagonal Spanish tower of St Nicholas so that it could take heavier armament, and it was garrisoned as part of the defences of Ciudadela.

Two of the towers defending Mahon, the St Clair and the Erskine Tower, were built on La Mola, the St Clair Tower being sited to prevent a landing in the bay of El Freus on the north side of the headland while the Erskine Tower defended the Cala Taulera, the stretch of water between La Mola and the Phillipet peninsula. A tower was also built on the eastern point of the Phillipet peninsula which today is called Isla El Lazareto. This tower was to provide flank protection for the defences of La Mola and to prevent an enemy obtaining access

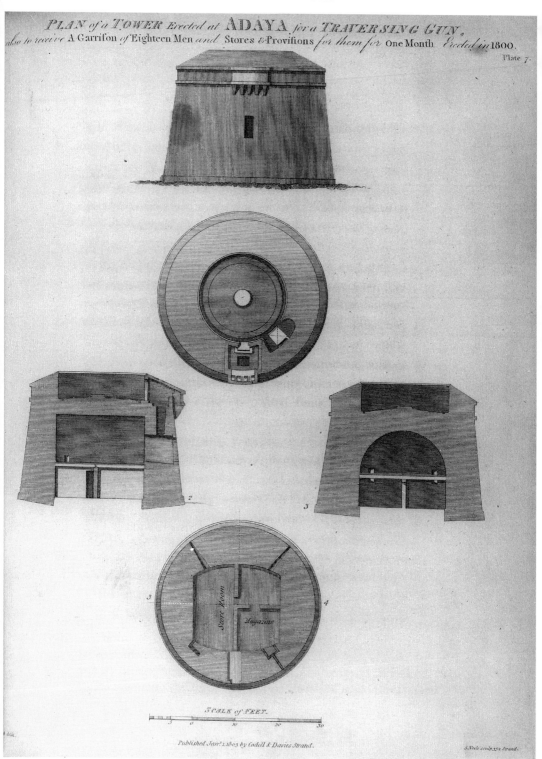

Published Janr 1.1803 by Cadell & Davies Strand.

The tower at Addaya on Minorca; from an illustration in Journal of the Late Campaign in Egypt, by Captain Thomas Walsh (1803). [British Library]

along the isthmus. The tower was supported in this role by an older Spanish one in the grounds of the Lazareto, a hospital which the British occupied and used as a barracks.

On the southern side of the harbour entrance were sited the main defences of Mahon, the massive Fort George, rebuilt in the ruins of the old Fort San Felipe, which had been destroyed by the Spanish after their recapture of the island in 1782, and the smaller Fort Marlborough across the inlet called the Cala San Esteve. To support these works a tower was built on the Sierra del Turco, a hill overlooking Fort Marlborough and linked to the fort by a stone wall which provided covered communication between the fort and the tower. This tower was named Mount Stuart Tower (Torre Penjat) and was built with the role of denying the hill to an enemy besieging Mahon, since on two previous occasions, in 1756 and 1782, batteries on this hill had been successful in making Fort Marlborough untenable. The tower was surrounded by a ditch and glacis which covered an angle of 180 degrees to the north while on the south, nearest the sea, there was no ditch but instead a battery protected by two walls.

The remaining towers, the construction of which was ordered in 1800, were planned to defend the main beaches and inlets north of Mahon at Addaya, Fornells and Sa Nitja. At Addaya, where the British had landed in 1798, a tower was built on the headland and two were built at Fornells, one on the headland at the entrance to the harbour and one on Sargantana Island in the middle of the harbour. A large tower was built at Sa Nitja to defend another inlet north-west of Fornells and, to the south of Mahon, two built by the Spanish in 1782, at Alcufar and Punta Prima, were refurbished and reused in a similar fashion to the St Nicholas Tower at Ciudadela.

The new towers were built under the direction of Captain D'Arcy, RE, the Commanding Engineer, assisted by a number of other officers, including Lieutenant Birch and Second Lieutenant Pasley. According to Pasley, writing almost twenty-five years later, ten of the eleven towers built by the British on Minorca were of two types, six being large towers and four small ones. The larger towers, Mount Stuart (Penjat), Phillipet (Felipet), Sa Mesquita, Fornells, Addaya and Sa Nitja were 36ft (11m) high with an exterior diameter of 55ft (17m). The smaller towers, Erskine (Los Freus), St Clair (Cala Taulera), Sa Torreta and the tower on Sargantana Island had a height of 30ft (9.25m) and an exterior diameter at the top of 35ft (10.75m).[4] Each tower had two floors and a gun platform with storerooms and a magazine on the ground floor together with a cistern for fresh water, though Captain Walsh of the 93rd Regiment, who visited the island on his way to Egypt in 1800, noted that there was a well in the tower at Addaya.[5]

All the towers were built of rubble masonry, but the larger ones, with the exception of the Phillipet Tower, had a feature not found in other British-built towers: following the example of the two earlier Spanish towers at Alcufar and Punta Prima, the British towers had a series of vertical columns of ashlar rising the full height of the tower and set into the rubble masonry at regular intervals around it and about 15ft (4.6m) apart. These columns served to reinforce the wall and gave each tower a distinctive striped appearance. The smaller towers and the Phillipet Tower did not have these columns but, instead, were completely faced with cut stone. The walls of the towers had a batter with a slope of either 1:12 or 1:15 beneath a cordon and parapet, and each tower, except those at Santandria and Sargantana Island, had a machicolation over the entrance. In the larger towers this machicolation was supported by five or more corbels while the smaller towers had a smaller machicolation supported by four corbels.

In the larger towers the entrance was through a short passage with an adjoining stone staircase built into the wall, which led up to the gallery of the machicolation and from there to the gun platform. In this respect they were similar to the later English towers, although these lacked a machicolation. In the smaller towers the short entrance

The Alcufar Tower, Minorca, built by the Spanish about 1782; it was used as a pattern for the later British towers on the island; the picture shows the original door at first-floor level and a ground-level door added later. [Author's collection]

passage was actually above the level of the first floor and the passage ended with a short flight of steps leading down into the first-floor living quarters. Access to the gun platform in these towers was through a small shaft about 2ft 6 inches (0.76m) square which led by means of a ladder to the gallery of the machicolation. This shaft could also be used to raise ammunition and powder to the gun platform and was also to be found in the larger towers where it was used specifically for this purpose. In both types of tower the ground floor was usually reached by a trapdoor and ladder from the first floor, but in the Mount Stuart and the Fornells Tower there was an open staircase built against the curve of the wall and similar to that used in the older Spanish towers.

The large towers were designed to mount a single heavy gun, a 24pdr, and there was space for a second smaller gun, usually a 5$\frac{1}{2}$in howitzer, using the same pivot. Eight howitzers were requested from the Board of Ordnance for the towers in 1800.[6] In an appreciation of the fortifications needed to defend Mahon Captain D'Arcy referred to the Lazareto Tower being designed to mount two guns on traversing platforms.[7] It is not clear whether by this he meant two 24pdr guns; but it is known that two 8in mortars were ordered for this tower in 1801, though it is unlikely that these were to be mounted on the tower.[8] The small towers each mounted a single heavy gun but the two older towers at Alcufar and Punta Prima retained their original arma- ment of four 12pdr guns each.

One feature included in the Minorcan towers was the provision of a recess in the parapet wall for a grate to heat shot to red heat for use against ships. Although the majority of towers simply had a grate Pasley says that in one tower a small brick furnace was built into the recess.[9] This feature was adopted in a number of Irish towers where a full-sized furnace was built into the parapet.

The similarity between the Minorcan towers and the early Irish ones constructed around Dublin and on Bere Island was not limited solely to the provision of shot furnaces. The design of the Irish towers closely resembled that of the tower at Addaya, and this is perhaps not so surprising since Birch, now a captain, and Lieutenant George Dyson, RE were both serving in Ireland in 1803 after previous service in Minorca, and Captain Birch was influential in recommending the use of towers for the defence of Ireland to the Commander-in-Chief, General Lord Cathcart. The Irish towers, built four years after the Minorcan ones, had a similar profile to the Addaya Tower, a machico- lation over the door and the same internal layout.[10]

Although ten of the eleven towers built on Minorca were generally similar in design, if not in size, one, that at Santandria, called in Spanish 'Es Castell', was very different from the others. Pasley specifically mentions it in his textbook on fortification and describes it to his students as being of particular interest. Only 26ft (8m) in height, it was surrounded by a dry ditch and glacis which reduced considerably that part of the tower visible above ground from a distance. The ditch was defended by a counterscarp gallery and a caponier, and entrance to the tower was not through a door at first-floor level, as in most of the other towers, but by the counterscarp gallery and the caponier. Around the top of the tower the parapet was extended and projected out from the wall supported by corbels with openings at regular intervals between the corbels to enable musketry fire to be brought on to an enemy at the base of the tower. The base was also protected by a further unusual feature, since the bottom floor of the tower was built 5ft (1.5m) below the level of the floor of the ditch. This floor contained a loopholed gallery running around the whole tower, enabling fire to be brought against an enemy who succeeded in entering the ditch. In this way the Santandria Tower was a forerunner of the larger Maximilian towers built some years later in Austria. One other, similar tower was also built by British engineers, on Bere Island in Ireland. The engineer responsible for this was Captain Birch and so it seems likely that he was responsible for the design of the Santandria Tower when he served in Minorca.

A number of the towers were subsequently modified, most by the Spanish after the departure of the British in 1802. One of those to be altered was the tower at Sa Mesquita, which was sited on a prominent

The tower at Sa Mesquita near Mahon; this is typical of the towers built by the British on Minorca but has increased protection at the rear of the gun platform added after 1802 to provide the gunners with cover from fire from the higher ground on the landward side. [Author's collection]

headland which itself was dominated by rising ground on the land-ward side. The later modification involved an increase to the size of the gallery of the machicolation above the door and building up and crenellating the rear parapet wall, also above the door, to protect the gunners from enemy fire from the high ground. It is uncertain whether this was a later British modification, possibly carried out when the British used the island again as a naval base later in the war - when once again the British and Spanish were allies - or whether it was carried out by the Spanish themselves. What is known, however, is that two Irish towers, at Knockalla and Dunree on Lough Swilly, both similarly dominated by adjacent high ground, were provided with almost identical protective walls at the rear of their gun platforms.

What is more certain is that the Spanish engineers changed the two smaller towers on La Mola and the two at Fornells. Those on La Mola, the Erskine and the St Clair Tower, were altered when the new Spanish fortress, Fort Isabel II, was built there in the 1850s. In each of these towers a large embrasure was opened in the wall at first-floor level for an additional gun to assist in providing flank defence for the new fort.[11]

The two towers at Fornells were also modified at a later date by the Spanish. The one on Sargantana Island was one of the smaller towers and was built to act as a keep for a small walled battery. The tower differed from the others built by the British in having its entrance at ground level and no machicolation. In order to strengthen the tower when a heavier gun was mounted on the platform, the Spanish engineers added two rectangular wings or small bastions each rising the full height of the tower to the parapet. These wings also provided additional protection for the ground-level entrance to the tower and they would appear to have been added after 1815 since Pasley did not mention the tower at Santandria as being in any way different in design from the others, and a Spanish inventory of the fortifications of the island dated 1805 described the tower then as being circular.

The Fornells Tower was adapted and reinforced to take two heavy guns on the platform, each traversing on a separate racer. The tower was reinforced by increasing the thickness of its wall, but, in particular, of the lowest third, which was given a pronounced batter to about 10ft (3m) above the ground and then rose vertically to an over-hanging, corbelled parapet which extended around the top of the tower. This reinforcement not only permitted the tower to mount a heavier armament than when it was first built, but it also increased its resistance to the more powerful artillery coming into service after 1820.

In addition to modifying some of the British towers, the Spanish built another one themselves after regaining possession of the island. This tower was built to defend the beach at Son Bou on the south coast and was constructed between 1804 and 1805. It was almost identical in design to the earlier Spanish towers at Alcufar and Punta Prima, but its life was brief. On 2 April 1808 a landing party from the frigate HMS *Imperieuse* (38 guns), commanded by Captain Lord Cochrane, RN, found the tower, if not unoccupied then certainly unarmed, and destroyed it by blowing it up. Today there is no longer any indication that the tower once stood, but the tactical importance of the headland on which it had been sited is clearly demonstrated by a concrete bunker built in 1936 during the Spanish Civil War which now stands in its place.

Today all the Minorcan towers, with the exception of Son Bou, still remain but in a state varying from the excellent to the partially demolished. Five - Mount Stuart, Phillipet, Sa Mesquita, Erskine and St Clair - are still owned by the Spanish Ministry of Defence, though Sa Mesquita Tower is now in the grounds of a privately-owned house. Mount Stuart, Phillipet and Sa Mesquita Towers are in relatively good condition, but those on La Mola are not. The internal floor and machicolation of the St Clair Tower have collapsed and Erskine Tower was partially demolished as the result of an explosion in 1957. Four of the remaining towers built by the British - Sa Torreta, Fornells, Sa Nitja and the tower on Sargantana Island - are privately owned, and the towers at Addaya and Santandria are owned by the local town councils. All except the tower at Addaya, the Sargantana Tower and that at Santandria are in poor condition. In recent years the Island Council of Minorca has initiated a policy of repairing and restoring some of them. The tower at Addaya was restored in 1973 and since then the Spanish-built tower at Alcufar has been repaired, as has that at Santandria, and there are plans to restore the tower at Fornells. This far-sighted policy to maintain these important relics of Minorca's heritage is much to be welcomed, and so far only in Canada and Mauritius have serious steps been taken on such a scale to save their remaining towers.

CHAPTER 5

The Towers in Ireland

The Early Towers

The threat of French invasion of the British Isles in the years 1795 to 1805 was not directed solely at England and Wales, but also at Ireland which was considered by Napoleon to be particularly vulnerable because of the civil unrest in the country at that time. The defence of Ireland presented particular problems because of the large number of possible landing places, especially on the west coast, to defend which would have required an immense number of troops and a vast expenditure on coastal fortifications. As in most situations, the answer had to be a compromise and the solution was to provide protection for Dublin and Cork, and for those anchorages such as Bantry Bay, Galway Bay, Lough Swilly and Lough Foyle which could give shelter to a fleet.

In December 1796 the French general Hoche and Wolfe Tone, the leader of the United Irishmen, a revolutionary Irish political party, had made an attempt to invade Ireland by landing in Bantry Bay in the south-west of the country with 15,000 men. Adverse winds prevented the force from landing and eventually caused the French fleet to disperse and return home. In August 1798 there was a further invasion attempt, this time rather more successful. Following the Irish rebellion in that year, another French general, Humbert, landed with a small force of a thousand men at Killala in County Mayo. Having defeated a British force of militia and yeomanry at Castlebar, Humbert crossed the Shannon north of Athlone but was eventually forced to surrender at Ballinamuck in County Longford. This invasion forced the British authorities to review their defensive plans and, in 1803, with England once again at war with France, Colonel Twiss was sent to Ireland to draw up a plan of defence for the country. He recommended that the main priority should be the defence of Dublin and that certain defensive positions should be established inland, including a number on the River Shannon.[1] The line of the Shannon now became the main defensive position to be held against any enemy landing on the west coast. Defences were built to cover the main crossings at Meelick, Keelogue and Banagher, while Shannonbridge, the nearest crossing point to Galway Bay, was strongly fortified with the only existing example of a *tête de pont* in Britain or Ireland.

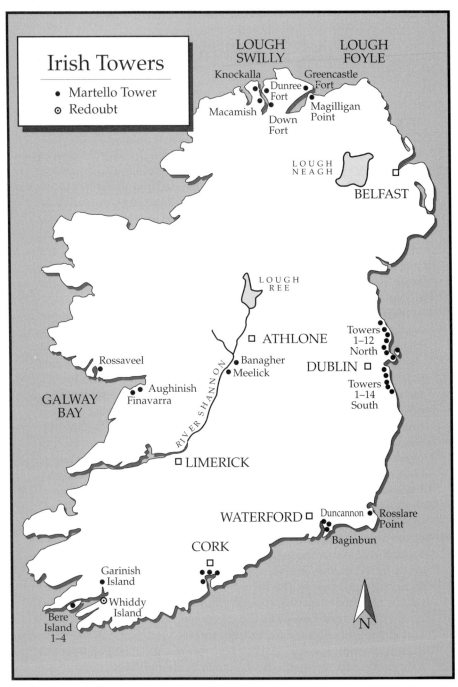

Map of the Irish towers. [Michael Pugh]

Ireland was not immune from the gun tower fever then sweeping through the English Military Districts and which even affected the Board of Ordnance. As early as 1803 the use of towers to defend vulnerable parts of the coastline had been proposed and this suggestion was given impetus by Captain Birch, RE who, it was said, had the ear of the general commanding in Ireland Lord Cathcart. Birch had, as we have seen, been involved in the construction of the Minorcan towers between 1799 and 1802 when stationed on the island, and he recommended the building of towers on Bere Island in Bantry Bay as early as May 1804.[2] Not all Birch's superior officers approved of his proposal and in a letter to Lord Sheffield, dated 20 December 1804, Colonel Henry Clinton, the Quartermaster-General in Ireland, complained, '...the Engineer, Captain Birch, your protegee *[sic]* who is a great favourite of Lord Cathcart and every Lady I meet, but with whom I cannot agree in his scheme of fortification, he is bit by Martello towers or defensible guard houses.'[3]

From Clinton's letter it is clear that Birch was submitting proposals for towers to protect landing places in Ireland at about the same time as Captain Ford was proposing them for the defence of the English south coast. It is also clear that he was not the only officer in Ireland 'bit by Martello towers' since a plan for towers to protect the coastline north and south of Dublin was already in hand before May 1804. Birch, however, did not approve of this, perhaps because he was not its author, advising Lord Cathcart that it would be better to fortify the capital since the coast defences could easily be turned by landings further north or south.[4]

The Irish towers were built in two main phases, the first between 1804 and 1806 and the second between 1810 and 1815 when war with the United States appeared imminent. The towers built during the first phase all resembled those built on Minorca four years earlier. This is perhaps understandable since the English south-coast design was still being considered by the Board of Ordnance at this date, and also because a number of engineer officers, then serving in Ireland, had previously served in the Mediterranean, including, as well as Birch and Dyson, Captain Debutts who had been with the expedition to Corsica. Subsequently, in the the second phase, towers were built to a number of designs including some to the English south- and east-coast designs and some, particularly those built to defend Cork harbour, to a quite new one.

Of the early towers the greatest number, twenty-six in all, were built around Dublin. Twelve were constructed between Balbriggan and Sutton Creek to the north of the city and fourteen more to the south from Sandymount to Bray. Altogether the line of them defended the coastline for 36 miles (57km).

The decision to build the Dublin Bay towers and those on Bere Island in Bantry Bay was made by Lord Cathcart himself. The decision regarding the Dublin towers resulted from a study of potential landing places in the Dublin area made by Rear-Admiral Whitshed. Admiral Whitshed had been appointed the naval adviser to the Lord Lieutenant of Ireland in 1802, with orders to superintend the arrangements for the defence of the coast and to organize the Sea Fencibles in Ireland. He advised Lord Cathcart on the siting of the towers and Cathcart sought agreement for their construction from Chief Secretary Wickham. In a letter of 29 May 1804 the commander of the forces was authorized by the Chief Secretary to take whatever steps were necessary to secure those parts of the coast between Drogheda and Wexford from an enemy landing,[5] and by 1 September construction of the Dublin towers was ordered under the supervision of the Commanding Engineer, Lieutenant-Colonel Fisher.

The towers were constructed as 'field works' to avoid the delays involved in submitting the plans to the Board of Ordnance, and this enabled work to be started on the Dublin towers in that September and for them to be virtually complete by December 1806, by which date they had been handed over to the Board of Ordnance.[6] So the Dublin towers were completed at least a year before those on the English south coast.

The tower at Sandycove, south of Dublin; perhaps the most famous of all Martello towers, it has now been restored and reopened as the James Joyce Museum. [Author's photograph]

The tower on Ireland's Eye Island, off Howth; this is one of the large 'double' towers which were armed with two 24pdr guns. [Author's photograph]

The Dublin towers bore a close resemblance to the Minorcan tower at Addaya, although four of them – those at Williamstown, Sandymount and Dalkey Island south of Dublin, and the tower on Ireland's Eye Island to the north – were larger and known in contemporary documents as 'double' towers. The northern towers were constructed of rubble masonry while those to the south were of granite in regular ashlar courses. The majority were about 24ft (7.3m) high with an external diameter at the base of 38 to 40ft (11.6 to 12.3m). As with the Minorcan towers, there was a machicolation over the doorway which was at first-floor level.

The 'double' towers, however, had a diameter of 50 to 52ft (15.3 to 16m) and differed externally in one or more respects from each of the other towers. The Sandymount one was closest in design to the majority of the smaller towers with a machicolation over the doorway and the bottom of the parapet marked by a string course. The Dalkey Island tower was similar to that at Sandymount but lacked the machicolation, while the other two towers - at Williamstown and on Ireland's Eye Island - were the only ones to have a projecting parapet supported by two continuous courses of corbels. The Ireland's Eye tower had the largest machicolation of them all and was supported by seven corbels, while the Williamstown tower had no machicolation at all. In its place were two openings in the corbel courses supporting the parapet one on each side of the door to enable musketry fire to be brought on an enemy attacking the entrance.

Each tower, except the one on Dalkey Island, had two storeys, a ground floor containing the magazine and store and a first floor providing the living accommodation. In 1861 a return reporting the accommodation available in each tower showed that those north of Dublin each had accommodation for sixteen soldiers while the southern towers accommodated only twelve. The battery and tower at Sandycove showed accommodation for thirty-six men, while the Dalkey Island tower was reported as having no accommodation at all. In none of the Dublin towers was accommodation shown for an officer. None of the towers had a central pillar supporting the gun platform, such as was to be provided in the later English towers, and, as originally built, there were no windows, only a number of ventilation shafts set at an angle in the wall sloping upwards. Access internally between each floor and the gun platform was by means of a stone staircase which was built into the thickness of the wall.

That the Dalkey Island tower had no accommodation was probably due to the fact that living quarters for the gunners manning the battery and the tower guns was provided in an adjacent guardhouse. The Dalkey Island tower differed from the majority of the others around Dublin Bay by having only a single internal chamber, the floor of which was only a few feet above the ground and under which was a small cistern. Entrance to the tower is shown in a section and plan of the tower dated 1868 as being through the parapet wall, and the Dalkey Island tower is the only Irish one known to have been entered in this way.[7] The chamber, or Gunner's Room as it was called, was divided into two unequal parts, the smaller forming two magazines separated by a central wall and with a door into each. Communication between the Gunner's Room and the gun platform was by means of the usual staircase within the wall. There was no machicolation, because of the parapet entrance, but built into the thickness of the wall there was a shaft, similar to those in the towers on Minorca, running down direct from the parapet to the Gunner's Room and which was used to move powder and shot to the guns.

The majority of the towers, both north and south of Dublin, were designed to mount one gun, but the four 'double' towers mounted two each. The northern towers were armed with 24pdr guns while the southern towers, with one exception, had the lighter 18pdr guns. The exception was the Dalkey Island tower, which was armed with two rear-pivoted 24pdr guns. All of the towers had a shot furnace built into the parapet. Eight of the fourteen southern towers had adjacent batteries but no batteries were built north of Dublin.

In 1803, when Colonel Twiss was sent to Ireland to advise on the defences, he was directed to examine, together with other locations, what security could be given to Bantry Bay. His report proposed the building of two large, casemated towers on Whiddy Island to protect the town and harbour of Bantry,[8] and a third on Garinish island in Glengarriff Harbour to the north of the town. Twiss's report was dated 15 January 1803 and by the following May the Inspector General of Fortifications, Lieutenant-General Morse, was asking for a sketch and description of 'The kind of round tower recommended in the report of the defence of Bantry Bay'.[9]

In the event three circular redoubts were built on Whiddy Island, it having proved impossible to cover the bay by fire from only two. They were similar in design to the redoubts built a year or so later at Dymchurch, Eastbourne and Harwich, but they lacked the casemates built under the terreplein which was a feature of the English redoubts. Instead the Whiddy Island fortifications had bomb-proof magazines and accommodation built in the centre of each redoubt. The largest redoubt in the centre of the island was armed with twelve guns and the two smaller flanking redoubts had eight each. All were complete by 1807.

In addition to the Whiddy Island redoubts and the Glengarriff Harbour tower already authorized by the Board of Ordnance, further fortifications were ordered by Lord Cathcart on Bere Island at the western end of Bantry Bay. Rear-Admiral Sir Robert Calder, who commanded the naval squadron based in Bantry Bay, wrote to the Rt Hon. William Wickham on 22 December 1803 to request protection for his victuallers and store ships, which were to be based at the Berehaven anchorage to supply his squadron.[10] Wickham agreed that protection for the ships was necessary and instructed Lord Cathcart to order his engineers to carry out the work. Cathcart accepted Captain Birch's proposal that four Martello towers and a redoubt should be constructed on Bere Island and these were also authorized by the Commander-in-Chief as 'field works'.[11] Work started on the towers in 1804 and by November of that year Lord Cathcart was able to report to the Lord Lieutenant that 'at Beer [sic] Island most of the works are ready for their guns' and that he expected the last of the works to be complete by Christmas.[12]

Birch's friendship with Lord Cathcart and his proposal for towers to defend Berehaven brought him into conflict with the Board of Ordnance. Birch had been sent to Bantry in January 1804 to super-vise the construction of the Whiddy Island redoubts, under orders from the Board, but Lord Cathcart requested the Commanding Engineer at Cork, Major Sir Charles Holloway, to permit Birch to supervise the Bere Island works and also advise on the defences of Dublin. Allowing Birch to supervise Lord Cathcart's 'field works'

brought both Holloway and Birch into an argument between the
Inspector General of Fortifications and the commander of the forces
in Ireland. The Inspector General believed that to allow Birch to leave
the supervision of the Board's works at Bantry was to set a dangerous
precedent, and he was supported in this view by the Master General
of the Ordnance. Lord Cathcart had no option but to accept this
ruling, but subsequently Birch was to leave Bantry in November 1805
to accompany Cathcart on his abortive expedition to north Germany.

The Bere Island towers were reported as ready on 2 February 1805
and were therefore probably the earliest Irish towers to be
completed.[13] The four, all circular in shape and built of rubble
masonry, were sited to defend the anchorage between the island and
the mainland and the small harbour of Lawrence Cove on Bere
Island. The dimensions of the towers vary, with Tower No.2, Cathcart
Tower at Rerrin, being 31ft (9.5m) in height with a parapet diameter
of 46ft (14.15m), while the Clochlann Tower, No.3, had a height of
26ft (8.1m) and a base diameter of 38ft (11.6m). Lieutenant Alcock,
RA, visiting Bere Island in 1824, wrote a detailed description of the
towers of which Cathcart Tower was particularly interesting. It was
surrounded by a ditch 14ft (4.3m) deep and on two sides of it was a
raised glacis under which, and unlike any other English or Irish tower,
were casemate barracks and a magazine. The barracks could accommodate a garrison of fifty men and from the casemates fire could be
brought all round the base of the tower and on the two sides of the
ditch not protected by a glacis. Access to the ditch was by a *pas de
souris,* that is a staircase, in the western edge of the sallyport. The tower
mounted two 24pdr guns and there were two 13in mortars sited 'in

*The Cathcart Tower at Rerrin on Bere Island, Bantry Bay; a watercolour by Lt A. Alcock, RA,
dated 1824.* [Courtesy of the Director, National Army Museum, London]

the glacis'. The armament of the other towers comprised two 24pdr guns on Tower No.1 and one 24pdr gun on each of the other two towers.[14]

In a number of respects the Cathcart Tower resembles the Santandria tower at Ciudadela on Minorca, in particular in the use of a glacis to reduce the amount of wall vulnerable to enemy fire. They were also similar in having protection for the ditch, provided in the Bere Island tower by the casemate barracks under the glacis, and in the case of the Santandria tower by a counterscarp gallery. This similarity in design between the two was probably no coincidence since Captain Birch, having served in Minorca, must have been familiar with the design of the Santandria tower and possibly even have been involved in its construction.

Although constructed at about the same time as the Bere Island towers, the decision to build the tower on Garinish Island in Glengarriff Harbour actually predated those on Bere Island, having been originally suggested in Colonel Twiss's report of 1803. It is possible that the Garinish tower may have been finished before the Bere Island towers but the report of the completion of the tower and the battery was not received by the Board of Ordnance until 14 August 1806. It is clear from drawings and comments made in 1808 by Lieutenant-Colonel Fenwick, the Commanding Engineer for the Cork District, that the original tower was of very inferior design and workmanship. It had a height of 25ft (7.6m) and a base diameter of about 37ft (11.3m), but the doorway was only 7ft (2.2m) above the ground and the door itself was placed at the chamber end of the entrance passage rather than being flush with the outside of the wall as in other towers.

Although there was a batter to the wall there were no windows nor loopholes and Fenwick considered the tower to be vulnerable to assault by a raiding party from an enemy ship and quoted the example of Lord Cochrane and the Spanish towers.[15] As first built, the tower did not have a bomb-proof arch supporting the gun platform but instead had only a wooden roof. This would not have been able to support a gun of any real size and weight, and in 1809 the armament of the tower was reported to be one 8in brass howitzer, an old-fashioned weapon which by that date was already considered obsolete.[16]

By 1811 the tower was in a poor structural state and Lieutenant-Colonel Fenwick wished to rebuild it using the same design as for the proposed Cork Harbour towers. This proposal to replace the old tower with a much larger one was rejected by the Inspector General of Fortifications on the grounds that the tower was only a keep for a battery and, as such, its then size was quite adequate for such a role.[17] In June 1811 a Committee of Engineers visited Bantry Bay and recommended that the tower and battery should be improved and strengthened and by April 1812 the tower was described in an inspection report as 'levelled to the ground' and this was also the state recorded in a similar report for the following year.[18] A further report in September 1816 indicated that the tower had been rebuilt and it would appear that Fenwick had used a modified design similar to that for the Cork towers since the Garinish tower, as it stands today, resembles these but on a reduced scale. The tower was still built of rubble masonry, like the ones at Bere Island, but now was drum-shaped with a vertical wall, a bomb-proof arch and, unusually, a base diameter rather less than the total height.[19]

By 1866 the tower was of little military use and Caesar Otway writing about the development of tourism in the Glengarriff area in the July issue of the *Irish Industrial Magazine* described it ironically:

> '*The Bay is studded with islands, on one of which the Government has been graciously pleased to erect a most picturesque Martello tower. One would think that Mr White (the local landowner), if such a thing were possible, had bribed the engineer, who located these fortresses, to build here - just by way of keeping in awe the herring fishermen - but in good faith to crown a prospect.*'

The fortification of Bantry Bay does seem to have been something of a panic measure, the efficacy of which was doubted by at least two professional officers. As early as 30 June 1803 Sir Charles Holloway, the engineer at Cork, wrote to Lieutenant-General Morse expressing his doubts about fortifying Whiddy Island and Bantry Bay, particularly as the nearest redoubt on Whiddy Island was 6,400yd (5,700m) from the battery on Garinish Island, and so one was unable to support the other.[20] Twenty years later, in 1824, Lieutenant Alexander Alcock, RA noted:

> '*Indeed it will long remain an enigma what object could have been in view in laying out not less than half a million of money in fortifying Bere and Whiddy Islands in Bantry Bay and leaving the bay of Adrigole between these two islands and completely out of reach of either open to the whole world.*'[21]

The final two towers to be constructed in this early period were built in County Wexford, at Baginbun Head and Rosslare Point. These were built as part of the chain of signal stations constructed on every headland from Dublin along the south and the west coast. In January 1804 the Lord Lieutenant, Lord Hardwick, proposed that 'Corsican Towers' should be erected at some of the locations in place of the proposed signal stations and defensible guardhouses, but it was decided to build towers only 'where it is supposed they will prove of more importance to the defence of the Coast'.[22] Only the towers at Baginbun Head, near Waterford, and Fort Point at Rosslare were built with the dual role of gun tower and signal station; both were complete by 1806.

Sir Arthur Wellesley, the future Duke of Wellington, visited both towers on a tour of inspection of the coast defences of the south and the south-west of Ireland, which he undertook in July of that year before taking up the post of Chief Secretary. Although only the Baginbun tower exists today it is probable that the two were similar in design. Wellesley describes them as very well built and recorded in his diary that the Baginbun tower was 'done by the same man who constructed the one on Fort point at Wexford'. He considered both towers to have 'a material fault' in having only a 24pdr carronade as armament and recommended that each should mount an 18pdr long gun.[23] The

The tower at Baginbun Point, Co. Wexford; completed in 1806, it was designed as a combined Martello tower and signal station; it was unusual in having four machicolations rather than just one as in the other Irish towers of that date.
[Author's photograph]

Baginbun tower was circular and similar in design to the Dublin Bay towers and was sited on a headland to defend a small beach at the entrance to Waterford harbour, but it was unusual in having four machicolations, one in each quadrant of the parapet. There is no record of the armament of the towers being changed as Wellesley recommended and this may be because, although built by the Army and taken over by the Board of Ordnance, they were manned by a Royal Navy lieutenant and a signalman and were most probably the responsibility of the Navy.

There was a pause in the building of the Irish towers between 1806 and 1810, though one tower was built north of Dublin, at Drogheda in 1808. The three-storey circular tower on top of the Millmount Hill was not a Martello tower but was described as a guardhouse for a battery of guns and was to act as a signal tower to communicate with the local Yeomanry regiments in the area. The two 9pdr guns which were mounted at the base of the tower behind a low wall dominated the town and, in particular, the bridge over the River Boyne in its centre.

This small fort could be used as a secure position for the garrison in time of civil unrest and had accommodation for twenty-five or thirty men with a small apartment for an officer. The tower had a diameter of 35ft (10.7m) and a height of 32ft (9.2m) and, as it was essentially a musketry tower, there was no gun platform on top but instead a slate roof rising from the wall of the upper storey. There was a line of large musketry embrasures at first-floor level and a second line of smaller loopholes in the wall of the floor above, which projected out from the lower wall supported on projecting courses. Above the doorway there was an opening in the course to act as a machicolation. In the *Topographical Dictionary of Ireland* (1837) it is referred to as Richmond Fort, having been named after the Lord Lieutenant at the time when it was built. By the 1950s the tower was in ruins, but since then its walls have been repaired and it stands today, an empty shell without its slate roof but still a dominating feature above the town.

1810 to 1815

The second phase of tower building in Ireland resulted from a report of the Committee of Engineers in Ireland which in 1805-06 considered what additional coastal fortifications were required to defend the country. Ireland was still unsettled after the 1798 Rebellion and the British authorities continued to fear the possibility that a French invasion force might evade the Royal Navy's blockade and attempt another landing in support of indigenous civil unrest. The west and the north-west coast were considered to be particularly vulnerable, but implementation of the Committee's proposals was delayed until the whole matter acquired a degree of urgency as a result of steadily deteriorating relations with the United States.

Towers were now proposed for the defence of possible landing beaches in Galway Bay, for the defence of the Shannon, for Duncannon in County Wexford, and for the shores of Lough Swilly and Lough Foyle in the north. Most of these later towers were built to the English east- and south-coast designs and it is clear from the adoption of these for use in Ireland that the Commanding Engineer was being encouraged to standardize tower design. The earlier towers in Ireland had been the responsibility of Brigadier-General Fisher and it was only in this second building phase that the English plans were made available for use in Ireland.

The use of the English plans was not yet insisted upon by the Board of Ordnance, who recognized that the Commanding Engineer should be allowed some freedom when selecting the appropriate design, but the Board's views on the matter were clearly stated in a memorandum from Major-Generals Mann and Twiss to the Inspector General of Fortifications, Lieutenant-General Morse. In the memorandum, dated 28 March 1810, the officers stated:

> '*There are no Plans for Towers here for two heavy guns; therefore if the mode adopted by Brigadier-General Fisher for mounting two guns on the Towers he has already erected in Ireland answer the ends proposed, and are not materially objected to by the officers of the Artillery, there can be no reason why that method should not be continued where two-gun towers are intended to be built. But there is another design of Tower lately adopted and generally approved here for one heavy gun (24pdr) and two smaller ones (24pdr short guns or 5$^{1}/_{2}$in howitzers) which construction it is presumed may be applied in many situations in Ireland with as much advantage as in England. It is therefore desirable that Brigadier-General Fisher should be furnished with Plans of these towers, to be adopted where it may be thought advisable.*'[24]

As early as 1804 proposals for the defence of the mouth of the Shannon and of the river itself had been considered since this was the major artery leading into the heart of the country and had been selected as the main defensive line for the defence of Dublin. In 1810, therefore, the decision was taken to reinforce the existing fortifications at the mouth of the Shannon, but these fortifications comprised batteries with defensible guardhouses rather than Martello towers.

In Galway Bay, however, three Martello towers were built between 1810 and 1812. Two of them mounted three guns and were built to the English east-coast design. The towers were each supported by a battery and were sited on a promontory on the southern shore of the bay. Both towers, the most westerly, Finnavarra Tower, and Aughinish Tower 3 miles (5km) further to the east of Finnavarra, were built of granite ashlar, the wall having a batter and four windows. In a barrack return of 1816 the accommodation at each tower was given as one officer and thirty soldiers, but this number almost certainly was not the number of those actually stationed there at that time and included the troops manning the guns of the battery.[25]

The third tower, at Rossaveel in Cashla Bay 20 miles (32km) from Galway Town, defended the only sheltered landing place on the northern shore. Also constructed of ashlar masonry, the Rossaveel tower appeared to be built to the English south-coast design, was elliptical in shape and mounted one heavy gun, a 24pdr, and one 8in brass howitzer. Unusually in this tower, the batter to the wall stopped about 6ft (1.8m) below the parapet, above which the wall then rose vertically. There was no masonry string course, which often marked the level of the gun platform in other towers. Internally the tower had no central pillar and so in a number of ways it was intriguingly different from the Kent and the Sussex towers it superficially resembled, and is a further example of the individuality of design which makes the Irish towers so interesting. In 1816 this tower had accommodation for one officer and twenty-eight men, a large number since here there was no supporting battery.

Since the Shannon was now the main defensive barrier behind which the government planned to defend against any invasion from the west, it became essential to defend the major crossing points on the river. Shannonbridge, north of Athlone, was already defended by a *tête de pont*, and Athlone itself was heavily fortified. Two crossings south of Athlone, at Banagher and Meelick, were reinforced with a Martello tower at each. A single-gun tower was erected to defend the

The Rossaveel Tower on the shores of Cashla Bay, Co. Galway. [Author's photograph]

bridge at Banagher, which was also protected by a seventeenth-century tower - Cromwell's Tower - which had been repaired and fitted out as a barrack and magazine with two 12pdr guns mounted on the top.[26] Fanesker Tower, as the Banagher Martello tower was named, was built to the English south-coast design, now the standard for a tower mounting a single heavy gun. The tower was elliptical in shape with its thicker wall facing to the north-west, the expected direction of attack and the armament was one 24pdr gun on a traversing platform.

At the ford at Meelick 5 miles (8km) downstream from Banagher, a three-gun tower was built, similar to the English east-coast design and to the two towers on the southern shore of Galway Bay. In 1804 defences had been planned at Meelick and in 1806 two batteries were noted in a list of land required for defence purposes.[27] So it is likely that the new tower was planned to reinforce the older works with its armament of one 24pdr gun and two howitzers or carronades.

The towers at Banagher and Meelick are examples of Martello towers constructed to defend a landward approach to a protected place rather than to provide coastal defence. Most contemporary writers on the subject of fortification did not favour the use of Martello towers to defend a position from land attack, despite Marshal Saxe's views on the use of such detached works. In Ireland, however, a number of towers, in addition to those on the Shannon, were built for just such a purpose, including two in County Wexford overlooking Waterford Harbour.

The main fortification defending Waterford Harbour was Duncannon Fort situated on the eastern side of the harbour and guarding a deep-water channel. The fort was an old one dating originally from the sixteenth century and it had been repaired and modernized over the years, but it was dominated by high ground 1,000yd (920m) to the north. Though the fort was well within the effective range of guns and howitzers positioned on the high ground, nothing had been done to secure the position. In 1811, however, the land was acquired by the Board of Ordnance and by 1814 work had commenced on building two single-gun towers, though they were not completed until after the war had ended in 1815. Once again the design used was that of the Kent and the Sussex towers but they were built with regular ashlar masonry rather than bricks. Although the towers were sited to prevent an enemy from taking the heights dominating the fort, their positioning was such as to place the thickest part of their walls to face the sea rather than to the north from which direction a land attack might be expected. Thus here at Duncannon the engineers seemed rather uncertain as to the exact role for the towers.

In his report of 1803 Colonel Twiss had also considered the defence of Lough Swilly in the north-west of the country. This deep sea lough, 15 miles (24km) in length, was considered an ideal naval anchorage, and a landing on the eastern shore would have placed an enemy within striking distance of the city of Londonderry. Measures were taken to fortify the lough with guns taken from the French warship *Le Hoche* captured by the Royal Navy when another invasion force, sent to support General Humbert, was repulsed off the coast of Donegal in October 1798. Two years later in their report of 1805-06 the Committee of Engineers recommended a number of fortifications in the north of Ireland, including additional works in Lough Swilly and and a new fort in Lough Foyle.

However, it was not until 1810 that it was decided to replace the existing temporary defensive works with these permanent fortifications and a number of towers were constructed on each side of the lough: at Knockalla Point, Dunree, Muckamish Point and on Inch Island, as well as batteries with defensible guardhouses at Rathmullen and Neid's Point near Buncrana. The guns from the *Le Hoche* were retained in use and moved to Knockalla where seven of them provided the main armament well into the middle of the century.[28]

The towers on the shores of Lough Swilly were all designed as keeps for batteries thus making them into substantial forts. At Muckamish Point, on the west side of the lough, a large circular tower, resembling the earlier Dublin Bay towers, was built originally to support a mortar battery although the armament of the battery was later changed to three 24pdr guns. Here may be seen a reversion to Brigadier-General

On the shores on Lough Swilly, Co. Donegal, the tower at Muckamish Point supported a battery of three guns; it is now a holiday home. [Author's photograph]

Fisher's original design for a tower mounting two heavy guns, indicating that at Muckamish, and also at Magilligan Point on Lough Foyle, the requirement was for a tower mounting two 24pdr long guns. So in these positions neither the English south-coast nor east-coast design, which had been used in Galway Bay and on the Shannon, was considered appropriate and there was still no suitable design for a two-gun tower available from the Board of Ordnance.

Knockalla Fort, or West Fort as it was originally named, had a cam-shaped tower on which was mounted one 24pdr gun and one 5½in howitzer. A cam-shaped tower, like the Knockalla tower, would usually have been armed with three guns, but in this case one of the gun positions on the platform was taken up by a small stone turret which covered the entrance to the staircase, which was not built into the wall as in other Martello towers. The tower was rebuilt in 1815 after a partial collapse, attributed, apparently, to poor work by the contractor, and it was probably after this that a crenellated wall was built at the rear of the gun platform to protect the gunners from fire from the high ground to the rear of the tower.[29] This addition is similar to a crenellation built on the Minorcan tower at Sa Mesquita, near Mahon. The Knockalla tower also had embrasures at ground-floor level covering the sunken road to the main entrance to the fort.

The tower at Down Fort on Inch Island resembled the one at Knockalla but mounted three howitzers, while Dunree, or East Fort, opposite Knockalla, originally had a circular redoubt built into the highest part of the rock on which the fort was built, rather than a tower. Dunree Fort was remodelled in 1810-15 and a low tower was built in place of the redoubt. Like the West Fort at Knockalla the East Fort was dominated by high ground behind it so the rear parapet wall was raised in a similar fashion to the tower at Knockalla to protect the gunners from fire from an enemy holding the high ground. This tower may be seen in a late nineteenth-century photograph taken shortly before the fort was again remodelled between 1894 and 1897.[30] In 1833 the armament of the fort was six 24pdr guns in the main battery and two 24pdr guns mounted on the tower; the height of the gun platform was said to be about 95ft (29.2m) above the sea.[31] The final rebuilding of the fort resulted from a further change in the policy for the defence of Lough Swilly, brought about by the introduction of modern, breech-loading, rifled guns. The new policy resulted in the demolition of the towers of both East Fort at Dunree and Down Fort on Inch Island.

The close defence of the city of Londonderry was provided by a fort and a Martello tower, one on each side of the entrance to Lough

The tower of West or Knockalla Fort on Lough Swilly, looking across to Dunree Fort on the opposite headland; the picture shows the additional height of the parapet at the rear which is similar to the added protection at Sa Mesquita on Minorca. [Author's photograph]

Foyle. On the Donegal side was Greencastle Fort with opposite to it a single tower at Magilligan Point in County Londonderry. Like the forts on Lough Swilly, the one at Greencastle had a tower which supported a battery of five guns. The Greencastle tower differed from most other Irish ones in being oval in shape with base dimensions of approximately 65ft (20.0m) by 48ft (14.7m) and a height of 50ft (15.3m). Only two other towers in Ireland, both in Cork Harbour, were also oval, but these had a more regular shape than the Greencastle tower which could best be described as being a squashed cam shape. Today the tower has two large embrasures at first-floor level each approximately 6ft (1.85m) high and 4ft (1.2m) wide, but at least one of them appears to be a later modification as a drawing of the tower dated 1856 shows only a small aperture where there is now an embrasure facing the sea.[32] Beneath the embrasure facing inland were a number of loopholes at ground-floor level which covered the approach to the main gate. In the arch of the embrasure above there was a smoke duct and it is possible that this large embrasure was designed to take a carronade to strengthen the defence of the main entrance.

The ground floor contained a magazine for the tower, but the fort's main magazine was on the lower level behind the main battery. The lower floor of the tower also contained a firing gallery, and access to this floor was by means of two trapdoors and ladders rather than by a staircase as in other Irish towers. However, there was a staircase linking the first floor with the gun platform on which two 24pdr carronades were mounted, and there was a shot furnace built into the parapet wall.

Built between 1812 and 1815, the tower at Magilligan Point was one of the last of the Irish ones to be constructed. It was a large tower with a diameter of 53ft (16m), a height of 36ft (11m) and had a wall 11ft (3.3m) thick, but there was no central pillar. The tower was designed to mount two 24pdr guns and this is probably why the design was once again a reversion to the earlier Irish pattern for a two-gun tower rather than the standard English east-coast one. It would seem that even as late as 1815 there still was no satisfactory Board of Ordnance design for a tower mounting two heavy guns. However, the Ordnance Survey *Memoir* of 1835 stated that at that date only one gun was mounted.[33]

The *Memoir* also stated that: 'In the centre of the tower there is an excellent spring', and in 1859 the well was calculated as holding 171 gall (376 litres) of water.[34] The tower retained a machicolation over the doorway and, as with the earlier Irish examples along the shores of Dublin Bay, had a staircase within the wall connecting the maga-

Magilligan Point tower on the Northern Ireland side of Lough Foyle; this was one of the last towers to be built in Ireland and was completed in 1815. [Author's photograph]

The shot furnace built into the parapet wall of the Sandycove tower. [Author's photograph]

zine on the ground floor with the gun platform on the top. Here too there was a shot furnace built into the parapet of the gun platform. The furnace had two entrances each with two steps down and with the furnace between. To enable the gun to continue to traverse, the racer was mounted on removable wooden blocks where it crossed the entrances to the furnace and the staircase.

Among the last towers to be built in Ireland were the five constructed between 1813 and 1815 to defend Cork Harbour. These had been recommended by the Committee of Engineers in Ireland as early as 1806 and their design was quite different from other English and Irish towers. Two, Rossleague and Haulbowline, were oval in section, but the others were circular and all were without a batter to the walls, giving them a drumlike appearance. All were faced with finely cut limestone ashlar and there was no machicolation over the doors. Three towers - those at Marino Point, Belvelly and Rossleague - were built on the northern shores of Great Island to protect the approaches to Cork Harbour from an attack from the landward side, covering as they did two fords and a bridge leading across to the island, while a large tower was built on Ringaskiddy Hill, on the western side of the harbour.

The Ringaskiddy tower was sited to prevent an enemy from taking the hill and bringing batteries to bear on Fort Westmoreland, the major fortification on Spike Island. This tower was described in a contemporary document as: 'A tower of the largest dimensions with ditch and glacis, for two 24pdrs, to be sunk as low as possible consistent with command of the ground around it.'[35] A fifth tower was on the highest point on Haulbowline Island, from which position it acted as a 'long stop', engaging any ship that might succeed in getting past Spike Island. With the exception of the tower on Ringaskiddy Hill, all the Cork towers were designed to mount a single 24pdr gun, but no old guns were available for use as pivots on the towers so attractive, six-pointed, star-shaped pivots made of cast iron were authorized, an example of which may be seen on Rossleague tower.

Although like the English towers none of those in Ireland ever fired a shot in anger, many remained in use until late in the nineteenth century. Some were retained as powder magazines and Manning Tower, at Marino Point on Great Island in Cork Harbour, was attacked in 1867 by members of the Fenian Brotherhood, an illegal

Map of Cork Harbour defences showing the arcs of fire from the forts and the Martello towers. [Michael Pugh]

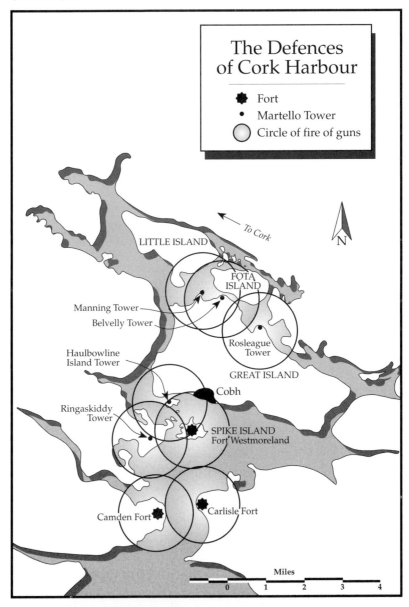

organization opposed to British policy in Ireland. The attack came
from a group of Fenians under their leader 'Captain Mackay', whose
real name was William Francis Lomasney. It was made just as the two
gunners who manned the tower were sitting down to their evening
meal with their families; the tower was captured without casualties or
a shot being fired. The Fenians escaped with all the stores and arms
held there and 300lb (131kg) of gunpowder from the magazine. This
was the only occasion that a British or an Irish Martello tower was
actually captured by an enemy; but it brought no luck to Lomasney
who died in 1884 in an ill-fated attempt to blow up London Bridge.

By 1887 a number of the Dublin towers had been sold or demolished. The one at Cork Abbey, south of the city, had disappeared by
1865 due to coastal erosion and seven others had been sold or
disposed of. Of these seven, three were subsequently demolished,
including two to make way for the Dublin and Wicklow Railway and
one, at Howth, was transferred to the Postmaster-General's depart-

*The tower on Haulbowline Island in Cork Harbour; the tower is still occupied by the Irish
Naval Service.* [Author's photograph]

ment to be used as the terminal for the cross-channel telegraph cables. North of Dublin four towers - those at Balcarrick, Rush, Drumanagh and Red Island - were handed over to the Coast Guard. The tower on Fort Point at Rosslare was endangered by erosion as early as 1819 and sold to the Wexford Corporation; by the following year it had been demolished. The towers of Down Fort, East Fort at Dunree, and Manly and Cathcart Towers on Bere Island were all demolished by the War Department at the end of the nineteenth century to make way for more modern coastal defences. The remaining Irish towers were retained for use by the War Department until beyond the end of the century.

The Towers Today

Today the majority of the Irish towers are still standing and of the twenty-six Dublin towers only five have fallen to erosion or developers. Those at Robswall, Portmarnock and Sutton Creek, north of Dublin, and Loughlinstown to the south, have been converted into houses with visually mixed results. Those at Portmarnock and Loughlinstown have each had an additional and rather ugly storey added to the gun platform, while the one at Robswall now resembles the tower of a French chateau. It has a tall, conical, slate roof, two levels of dormer windows in the roof, a tall chimney and, at ground level, a high crenellated stone wall has been built on either side of the tower. Only the tower at Sutton Creek has managed to retain most of its original features without alteration, although a sun room, similar to those on Towers 60 and 62 in England, has been added.

The remainder of the Dublin towers exist in conditions varying

Tower 5, north of Dublin, also known as Hick's Tower; it has now been converted into a house.
[Author's photograph]

from good, as in the case of the Sandymount, Seapoint and Williamstown towers, to derelict as at Balbriggan and Drummanagh. In addition, one tower, that at Sandycove, has been restored to its original condition and is open to the public. This tower was leased in 1904 by the Irish surgeon and wit Oliver St. John Gogarty for a rent of £12 per annum and was the setting for the opening chapter of James Joyce's book *Ulysses*. It has now been converted into the James Joyce Museum and is visited by thousands of people each year.

Outside Dublin the tower at Baginbun Point and one of the two at Duncannon, both in County Wexford, together with those at Muckamish Point and Knockalla on Lough Swilly are all occupied. The Baginbun tower was purchased by the local parish priest after the Second World War with the intention of using the stones of the tower as building material. Happily, this did not happen and the tower was sold again to the father of the present owner. The tower has been sympathetically converted and the additional living accommodation has been built alongside it. Muckamish and Knockalla towers have been allowed to remain, externally at least, in their original state although a wooden accommodation extension to the Muckamish tower has been built in the battery area.

Elsewhere in Ireland the remaining towers are empty and derelict, with the exception of Greencastle Fort and the tower at Magilligan Point on Lough Foyle, the tower on Haulbowline Island in Cork harbour and the tower on Garinish Island, near Bantry, also in County Cork. Greencastle Fort has been an hotel for many years and the present owner has been renovating the old living quarters of the fort to provide modern hotel accommodation, but the tower is used as a store. On the opposite shore of the lough the Magilligan tower has been restored by the Northern Ireland Department of the Environment but, unfortunately, because of financial constraints, it is no longer open to the public. The tower on Haulbowline Island is used by the Irish Naval Service and this tower, together with Towers 14 and 15 at Hythe in Kent and the Fort Frederick Tower in Canada, are the only ones still used by the military.

The tower on Garinish Island has probably the loveliest situation of all the towers, sited as it is in the middle of the beautiful Glengarriff Harbour. In 1910 the island was converted into a magnificent Italianate garden, designed by Harold Peto for its new owner Annan Bryce, a Belfast businessman, and named by him 'Illnacullin'. The Martello tower has become a feature of the garden, rather as Caesar Otway predicted in 1866, and the garden and the tower are now maintained by the Irish Board of Works.

CHAPTER 6

The Channel Islands and Scotland

The Channel Islands

'little bit of France cast into the Channel and gathered up by
England' was Victor Hugo's description of the Channel
Islands. It is this proximity to France, England's traditional
enemy in the eighteenth and the nineteenth century, which explains
the vast number of castles, forts and towers which fortify the
coastlines of these islands.

It was France's alliance with the rebellious American colonists in
1778 that caused the Jersey authorities to consider fortifying the
whole coastline, and in that year General Conway, the Lieutenant
Governor, proposed that thirty-two 'Towers of masonry with corre-
sponding batteries' should be built around the coast of the island.[1]
Construction of the first four started in 1779, but in 1781 there was
a dramatic spur to the construction programme when a soldier of
fortune, the Baron de Rullecourt, led an invasion of Jersey by French
troops. The Baron was defeated in the streets of St. Helier in what
came to be called 'The Battle of Jersey', but the very fact that the
French had been able to land emphasized the need for improved
coastal batteries and beach defences.

Twenty-three of these pre-Martello towers were built between
1778 and 1801, covering almost all of the coastline of Jersey except
along the north. It seems possible that the towers were designed by
General Conway himself but originally built under the direction of
the Commanding Engineer, Captain Frederick Bassett, RE. The
towers were sited approximately 500yd (450m) apart and in appearance resembled the Spanish atalayas or watchtowers, and perhaps
once again reflected the Spanish influence on British military engineering resulting from the eighteenth-century occupation of Minorca.
The design of the towers was quite different from that of the later
Martello towers, all but one of those on Jersey being circular. The
exception was the Seymour Tower in Grouville Bay which was square.
Although their height, 36ft (11m), was similar to that of the Martello
towers, their base diameter was smaller. There was no batter to the
wall and all but the Seymour and the Archirondel Tower had four
machicolated galleries projecting from the parapet. In some cases it

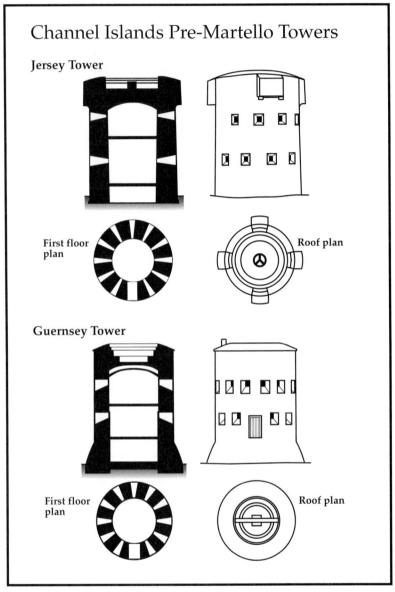

Channel Islands Pre-Martello Towers

Jersey Tower

First floor plan

Roof plan

Guernsey Tower

First floor plan

Roof plan

Comparative drawing of Jersey and Guernsey towers. [Michael Pugh]

would seem that these machicolations were later additions as in his 'Remarks on the Defences of the Island of Jersey', dated 25 November 1802, Major John Humfrey, RE, the Commanding Engineer on the island, noted that 'few towers have machicoules'.[2] The Seymour Tower was never provided with a machicolation, but Archirondel Tower had three double machicolations each covering an angle of wall of 120 degrees.

Each tower was pierced with musketry loopholes on two floors and access to the upper floors was by means of ladders. Although the towers were originally designed to provide only musketry fire in support of defending troops entrenched nearby, General Conway had envisaged an 'amusette', or wall piece, mounted on the roof platform. It is uncertain whether the 'amusettes' were ever mounted but it is known that the towers did mount small coehorn mortars. Humfrey recommended in his 'Remarks' that a single 18pdr carronade should be mounted on a special platform and this was done. This specially adapted, traversing platform had its wheels at each end placed on racers mounted on the wall of the tower rather than the gun platform, so ensuring that the whole weight of the gun and traversing platform was placed on the wall of the tower rather than on the roof. This partic-ular design was necessary because there was no central pillar sup-porting the roof, and also because of the limited space available on the roof platform for a traversing plat-form, even for a carronade.

Three towers - La Rocco standing on an islet half a mile out to sea in St. Ouen's Bay, Archirondel Tower in St. Catherine's Bay and Seymour Tower in Grouville Bay - each had a gun platform for a battery at the foot of the tower. The Archirondel battery comprised four 18pdr guns, the Seymour Tower had two 12pdrs (which were later replaced by two 24pdr guns). The battery of the La Rocco Tower, the last of the pre-Martello or 'Conway' towers to be built and completed in 1801, was much more powerfully armed, mounting five 32pdr guns. The majority of the other towers had earth batteries built in close prox-imity, but these rapidly fell into

Le Hocq Tower, Jersey; the Jersey towers had a batter for the full height of the wall and four machicolated galleries. [Author's photograph]

disrepair after 1815, and by 1859 these towers remained unsupported by batteries and six, in Grouville Bay, were described at that date as 'Musketry towers'.[3]

Within days of General Conway's being authorized to start building his towers on Jersey, authority was also granted for the construction of fifteen towers on Guernsey 'of the same form and mode as those ordered for the Island of Jersey'.[4] Captain Bassett was sent to Guernsey to supervise the building and so it may be fair to assume that the Guernsey towers were built to the original Jersey design while the latter design was altered to allow for a retrospective addition of machicolation. Certainly Bassett was ordered to leave with his successor, Captain Mulcaster, RE, the plan and section of the Jersey tower which implies that initially the towers on the two islands were similar.

The Guernsey towers differed from those on Jersey in being slightly smaller, with a thinner wall and no machicolation. In addition, unlike the Jersey towers, the walls of the Guernsey towers had a pronounced batter for the first 8ft (2.5m) and then rose vertically. Originally it was planned that each would mount one coehorn mortar firing from the roof platform, but at a later stage the roof was strengthened to mount a 12pdr carronade on a specially constructed, traversing platform. A number of towers, including Rousse Tower (Tower No.11) and Mont Crevelt (Tower No.3), were reinforced in 1805 by the construction of adjacent batteries making them much more effective fortifications.

Fort Grey, Guernsey; built in 1804-05, this is sited on an islet in Rocquaine Bay and was designed as a keep for a battery. [Author's collection]

These early towers on Guernsey were criticized in 1787 by the Committee of Engineers which doubted their effectiveness, and in 1804 three further towers were requested by the Lieutenant Governor, Sir John Doyle, and were provided by the States of Guernsey, so avoiding Board of Ordnance scrutiny of the plans and speeding up construction. Designed to act as keeps for batteries surrounding them, these were smaller than the English south-coast towers and mounted a single 24pdr carronade on the gun platform specifically to defend the battery from infantry attack. All three forts were similar in design, but the tower of Fort Grey was larger than those of Fort Houmet or Fort Saumarez. Only the tower of Fort Grey had a central pillar and, while all three had the usual first-floor entrance, Forts Houmet and Saumarez each had an exterior stone staircase up to the doorway. In 1805 the workmanship of the towers was severely criticized by Captain Mackelcan, RE who commented:

> *'The third tower constructed at the Humette considered in any other light than a mere guardroom could not have been placed or constructed more injudiciously in my opinion.'*[5]

Despite Mackelcan's disparaging remarks, all three towers remained part of the island's defences until the latter half of the last century. In 1852 the battery armament of all three forts was partially modernized by replacing some of the 24pdr guns with 8in shell guns and more powerful 32pdr guns. All three towers may still be seen today and Fort Grey is now a maritime museum. However, most of the lower battery of Fort Saumarez has been demolished and the tower itself is now surmounted by a four-storey, German concrete observation post from the Second World War.

Four years later building work on a further three towers was started in Jersey. Similar in design to the later Guernsey towers but without the surrounding gun platform and wall, these were complete by 1814. They were sited to cover gaps in the original line of towers with one on Ile au Guerdain in Portelet Bay, another, the Icho Tower, in St. Clement's Bay and the Tour de Vinde on Noirmont Point. The armament of the Tour de Vinde was a single 18pdr gun on top of the tower with a second 18pdr at the base

Fort Saumarez, Guernsey: seen here with a four-storey, concrete observation post built on top by the German Army in the Second World War. [Author's collection]

sited to provide enfilade fire across St. Aubin's Bay towards Elizabeth Castle. The Portelet Bay tower, however, was a smaller and much inferior one, really more of a guardhouse than a Martello tower. With a diameter of 27ft (8.27m) and a height of 17ft (5.2m), it was rather roughly built of rubble stone. There was a single window about 7ft (2.15m) above the ground and the door was at ground level. The armament was one 18pdr carronade, and the garrison consisted of a sergeant and twelve men.

Icho Tower was a much larger one than the Tour de Vinde at Noirmont and, with a base diameter of 42ft (13m) and a height of 39ft (12m), it was as large as the English south-coast towers, although circular in shape. Sited on the rocks of the Banc du Violet 1 mile (1.62km) offshore from the south- east corner of the island, the tower was designed to support the Seymour Tower and its battery of two 12pdr guns a mile or so to the east. Together the two defended the channel to Platte Rocque and the construction of the Icho Tower seems to have been a belated strengthening of the defences covering the approach used by Baron de Rullecourt when he landed on Jersey in 1781. This granite ashlar tower was armed with one 24pdr gun on the gun platform.

By 1830 most of the defences of Jersey had fallen into disrepair as both the States of Jersey and the Board of Ordnance were reluctant to spend money on their upkeep. In 1831 the Commanding Engineer, Lieutenant-Colonel Lewis, RE, submitted a report to the Inspector General of Fortifications requesting authority to repair and modernize certain of the defences and to build further works. As a result of his submission, modernization was authorized and financial responsibility for the island's defences regularized. The Board assumed responsibility for the defences on the east, the south and the south-west coast and the States of Jersey took responsibility for those on the west, the north-west and the north coast. Lewis's report resulted in the construction of the final five Martello towers on Jersey.[6]

The original proposals were for a three-gun tower, subsequently to be called Kempt Tower after the then Master General of the Ordnance General Sir James Kempt, to replace a battery of three guns sited between L'Etacq Point and a new 'North Battery', and a second three-gun tower to be sited on the conical hill at the end of L'Etacq Point. The Inspector General of Fortifications did not accept Lieutenant-Colonel Lewis's view that a three-gun tower was necessary for this position, particularly as there was a difference of £1,300 between the estimate for the three-gun tower and that for a smaller single-gun one, and so only the smaller tower mounting one 24pdr gun was autho-

Kempt Tower, Jersey, built to a standard English east-coast design in 1834. [Author's photograph]

rized. Kempt Tower was built further south in St. Ouen's Bay; completed in 1834, it was built to the standard English east-coast design, mounting one 24pdr gun and two 24pdr short guns.

A second three-gun tower, La Collette, at Pointe des Pas was also built in 1834 to defend the Havre des Pas area beneath the flank of Fort Regent. This had been recommended as early as 1808 by Major Humfrey and, like Kempt Tower, was cam-shaped and built to the English east-coast design.[7] Two further towers were built: Lewis Tower in 1835 and, finally, Victoria Tower in 1837. These last two were small towers mounting one 24pdr gun each. Lewis Tower was in St. Ouen's Bay, sited between Kempt Tower and the older La Rocco Tower, while Victoria Tower was built above Mont Orgueil Castle at Gorey to defend Ann Port and secure the high ground above the castle.

The three single-gun towers resembled in design those built on the island in the period 1808-14, being circular and with a slight batter to the wall. Although all were apparently designed under the initial supervision of - if not actually built by - Lieutenant-Colonel Lewis, the three towers, superficially similar, actually differed in a number of important ways. Lewis Tower, having a larger base diameter than L'Etacq Tower, had a central pillar supporting the gun platform while, unusually, L'Etacq Tower had a base diameter less than its height, which gave it a tall, narrow appearance, and this was probably why no central pillar was required. The width of the front section of the wall in both towers was slightly thicker than that of the rear section: in the case of the Lewis Tower the difference was 1ft (0.3m) but in L'Etacq Tower it was double that. Victoria Tower was the only tower on Jersey to be surrounded by a ditch which was 12ft (3.69m) deep and 10ft (3m) wide. The tower was entered across a small drawbridge beneath which, in the counterscarp, was a small, recesssed room with two doors which might possibly have contained a shot furnace, although more likely it was an additional store. All the towers had a stone staircase linking the three floors and mounted a 24pdr gun.

Today four of the five later towers still remain. L'Etacq Tower was used as an artillery target and destroyed by the German Army during their occupation of Jersey in the Second World War. La Collette Tower, appropriately perhaps, has been absorbed into the nineteenth-century Artificers' Barracks and Workshops which have been modernized and now house a Royal Engineers unit of the Territorial Army. Victoria Tower has been acquired by the National Trust for Jersey and Lewis Tower remains unused but in good condition, the responsibility of the Public Services Committee of the States of Jersey. Kempt Tower is now used as an interpretation centre provided by the National Trust for Jersey which has refurbished the tower. The centre tells the story of the conservation of the wildlife area called Les Mielles de Morville and the history of the tower. It is visited by hundreds of people each year.

Although only the later Jersey towers resemble the English Martello towers, the earlier ones are still referred to in the Channel Islands as 'Martello' towers. Their design reflects local circumstances and in the three types of tower on the Islands it is possible to see the logical progression from watchtower to almost impregnable gun tower.

The Victoria Tower, Jersey: the only tower in the Channel Islands to be surrounded by a ditch.
[Author's photograph]

Scotland

In Scotland, safely far from France, it was a different situation since there was little threat of invasion. Rather the threat was from commerce-raiders and this became particularly so when war with the United States was declared in 1812. Protection of the assembly areas for the Baltic and Scandinavian convoys became a matter of prime importance, since it was these that brought back the bulk of the masts and other naval stores so vital to the Royal Navy. In 1807 the Board of Ordnance proposed that a tower 32ft (9.8m) in diameter, built of ashlar blocks and mounting one or two guns, should be built on Beacon Rock, an islet at the entrance to Leith Harbour, the port for Edinburgh. In this case, unlike the procedure used when constructing other towers, the Board's proposal was to provide the finance for the tower and other defences, but the actual construction was to be carried out by the Edinburgh City Corporation. This proposal was accepted by the Corporation and there then developed a saga of procrastination and sharp practice which did not see the tower actually completed and handed over to the Board of Ordnance until thirty years later.

It would appear that it was Major Alexander Bryce, RE, the Commanding Engineer North Britain, who suggested that the Edinburgh Corporation should build the tower. In a letter to Captain Birch, RE (the same Birch who had built the towers on Bere Island and who was shortly to be Bryce's successor in Scotland), Bryce wrote: 'I have arranged matters so as to get the Beacon Rock Tower executed by the Corporation which will save us a great deal of trouble and expense in water building.' In the same letter he went on to describe the initial design for the tower which was to have 'A curve the better to resist & break the force of the waves... after the principle of the Eddystone Light house'.[8] It was to be 52ft (16m) high, although only 36ft (11m) would be above the water level, with a base diameter

The tower at Leith, near Edinburgh; this very large tower is now partly encased in the breakwater and pier built by the Leith Harbour Board in 1937. [Author's collection]

of 44ft (13.5m) and with a gun-platform diameter of 32ft (9.8m). There was to be just a single, square, central chamber built over a low basement and there would be no central pillar to support the bomb-proof arch.

It would also seem that the construction of the Leith tower was a project in which the Master General of the Ordnance took a partic-ular interest. Bryce indicated as much to Birch when he wrote: 'The Master General is desirous of forwarding this business, which I believe he had promised when in Scotland, I will therefore hint to you *entre nous* that any facilities you may afford it will be acceptable to him & not thrown away.'[9] Birch was unsuccessful in spurring on the Edinburgh Corporation to start work on the tower and the Inspector General of Fortifications, Lieutenant-General Morse, became irri-tated by the delay, feeling that the Corporation was not expending to the best advantage the funds made available by the Board of Ordnance. In 1810, believing that he would have the support of the Master General, Morse improved and enlarged the design without the prior approval of the Board, increasing the diameter to almost 80ft (24.6m) and the height above water level to 45ft (13.8m). The gun platform was redesigned to mount three heavy guns and the final esti-mated cost rose dramatically. The Inspector General had, on this occasion, overestimated the support he would receive from the Master General, probably because of the enormous increase in the cost of the tower, and he was sharply reprimanded by the Board; but the new design was accepted.

The final cost of the tower rose to £17,179.18s.4½d, but by 1828 a report stated that the interior was still incomplete and that 'The tide ebbs and flows through the tower by pipes fixed in the lower storey.'[10] There was no well nor cistern in the tower and the storerooms and a magazine could be provided only if the lower storey could be made watertight. The tower was not taken over by the Board of Ordnance from Edinburgh Corporation until 1838 and even then it was not complete. Nor was it complete ten years later when the *Inspection of Forts, Towers and Batteries* for Scotland for that year reported: 'The masonry is very good but the Leith Tower has never been finished, and is indeed a mere Shell of Stonework into which the sea flows from 12 to 15ft [3.6 to 4.6m] deep every tide, and is altogether Useless.'[11] However, a similar report for the year 1853 indicates that the situation had improved. By then the tower was reported as being constructed for three 32pdr guns with accommodation for one officer and twenty-one soldiers, and was 'In good order and fit to receive troops'[12] Despite the fact that the tower was, at last, complete the report showed that no guns had been mounted by that date and, indeed, the tower was never armed.

Between 1936 and 1943 a new deep-water harbour at Newhaven was incorporated into Leith Harbour, and part of this development was a further extension of the East Pier. This extension took in the Martello tower, where it remains today, part of the pier, boarded up and in deteriorating condition.

Two other towers were erected in Scotland. In 1813 the Secretary of the Baltic Association, worried about the depredations of American

Section of the tower at Hackness on Hoy in the Orkney Islands. [PRO MPH 620/5]

privateers, wrote to the Secretary to the Admiralty J.W. Croker regarding the need for protection for the ships of the Baltic trade which gathered in Longhope Sound on Hoy in the Orkneys while awaiting a convoy. 'Sir', he wrote, 'I am directed by the Liverpool Baltic Association to suggest to you the hazard to which the Trade is subject while lying at Long Hope Sound waiting for a convoy.'[13] The Admiralty promptly passed the request for protection to the Board of Ordnance, explaining that Their Lordships did not wish to station a warship at Longhope. It would be much preferable, the letter stated,

> *'both in point of economy and convenience... that a battery of a few heavy guns on one of the points commanding the entrance of the sound be put under the charge of a Non-Commissioned Officer and two or three Artillery men to be assisted by the seamen of the ships in case of attack.'* [14]

The Board of Ordnance, despite not being entirely certain where exactly Longhope Sound was and leaving that detail to the Commanding Engineer North Britain, who was presumed to know that sort of thing, authorized the construction of a battery of eight guns and two Martello towers. These towers, 47ft (14.4m) in diameter and 33ft (10.1m) high, were of the standard English south-coast design, but were built of sandstone ashlar rather than brick. Each tower cost £5,264.16s.2½d and mounted one 24pdr gun. The dimensions of the wall of the tower were 9ft 6in (2.9m) at its thickest, to the front, permitting a staircase to be built within the wall, and narrowing to 6ft 3in (1.92m) at the rear. Within the parapet wall were the usual recesses for ammunition and, unusually, sanitary provision for the garrison was also made by providing a urinal built into the parapet linked to an external pipe.

The eight-gun battery was built close to the Hackness tower and construction of the towers and battery began later in 1813. However, as was the case with many Martello towers, they were not completed until after peace was signed in 1815. By the 1840s the towers and the battery were shown in reports as being disarmed and it was not until 1866, when many of the coastal fortifications were undergoing modernization, that the decision was taken to rearm the defences of Longhope Sound. More powerful 68pdr guns were installed, which necessitated some refurbishment of the towers to take these larger guns. The towers are still to be seen today at Hackness and Crockness, the two headlands at the entrance to the sound, and the Hackness tower, which served as a naval signal station in the First World War, is now in the care of Historic Scotland and open to visitors.

CHAPTER 7

Canada 1796 to 1815

ogether with Ireland, Canada was another part of the British Empire where Martello towers were built in some numbers. As with the Jersey towers, there were three distinct building periods. A total of sixteen towers were built: three between 1796 and 1798, seven between 1810 and 1815 and a further six almost thirty years later. Three were built at Halifax between 1796 and 1798, and these towers, although not Martello towers in the purest form, were among the earliest Martello-type towers to be built. Their construction was authorized by HRH Prince Edward, the Duke of Kent, commander of the British forces in Nova Scotia and son of King George III. Prince Edward was determined to bring the old defences at Halifax to a state where they could resist French attack and the three towers were built under the budget heading of 'field works' thus, once again, avoiding the need to obtain the prior approval of the Board of Ordnance for their design and construction.

Work on the first tower, the Prince of Wales Tower, commenced in 1796 but was halted in November of that year on instructions from

Map of Canada. [Michael Pugh]

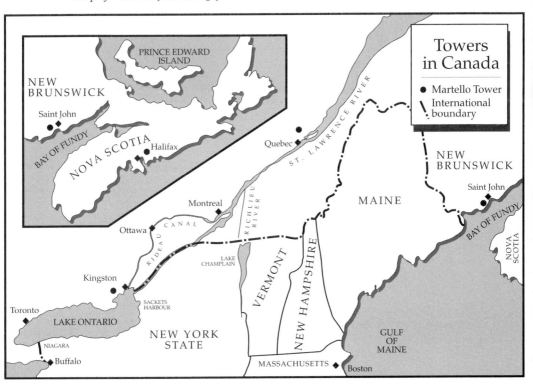

London on the grounds that the stone tower constituted a permanent defence work rather than a temporary field work. Prince Edward's influence at home was sufficient to ensure that work was only briefly halted and *ex post facto* approval for construction of the tower was received in June 1797 and work restarted.[1] By 1798 two other towers had been completed as keeps for redoubts and these were named after Prince Edward's brothers, the Duke of York and the Duke of Clarence.

The Prince of Wales Tower, sited on Mount Pleasant in front of the Citadel and designed to protect the three principal batteries defending the harbour from attack from the rear, was much larger than a normal Martello tower. The diameter was 72ft (22m) and, although it was only 26ft (8m) high, it was designed to hold a garrison of up to 200 men. The tower was constructed of rubble masonry and there was a slight batter to the wall. Unlike an English Martello tower, the Prince of Wales Tower originally had a thick timber roof which was not bomb-proof nor, ultimately, even waterproof. The roof provided a gun platform 60ft (18.46m) in diameter and was itself supported by a hollow, circular, masonry pillar which formed a narrow central room on each floor.[2]

Plan, elevation and section of the Prince of Wales Tower at Halifax, Nova Scotia; these drawings show the tower before it was rebuilt in 1810. [PRO MPH 491(6)]

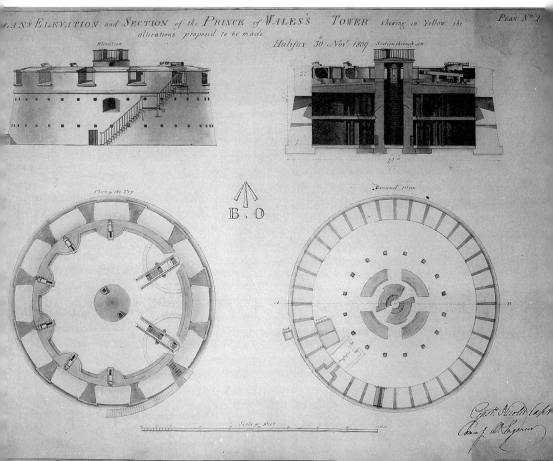

The Duke of Clarence Tower and the Duke of York Tower were considerably smaller in   diameter than the Prince of Wales Tower, being 50ft (15.4m) and 40ft (12.3m), respectively, but 42ft (12.9m) and 30ft (9.25m) high. The Duke of Clarence Tower was situated within the Duke of Clarence Redoubt and had three storeys rather than the two in the other two towers. It was surrounded by a ditch which was protected by two loopholed caponiers extending from its base. The Duke of York Tower, also sited within a redoubt, was on a high bluff overlooking the outer harbour. As in the other towers, it had no solid central pillar to support the gun platform. Instead the roof was supported by a hollow, circular masonry pillar similar to that in the Prince of Wales Tower and once again forming a narrow room extending the entire height of the tower. The Duke of York Tower was unique in having a timber parapet projecting over the wall and forming a machicolated gallery around the tower.[3] The Prince of Wales Tower and the Clarence Tower, having been built with musketry embrasures at ground and first-floor level, were not provided with machicolation.

When the towers were first built access to all three, together with communication between the several levels within them, differed from the arrangements in the English towers constructed ten years later. Access to the Prince of Wales Tower was by means of an external wooden staircase to the parapet built against the wall and then through one of the twelve gun embrasures. The staircase consisted of two flights with a short retractable landing between them which could be withdrawn into the wall of the tower, so acting as a drawbridge. Within the tower each floor could be reached by means of a staircase built inside the central hollow pillar.

Clarence Tower was sited within a surrounding redoubt and entrance was at first-floor level which, in actual fact, meant that the door was on the same level as the terreplein of the redoubt. As with the Prince of Wales Tower, access to the York Tower was through the parapet by means of an external staircase; but here there was a small drawbridge operated from the parapet itself and reaching to a most unusual wooden staircase comprising two flights of stairs which were free-standing away from the side of the tower. As in the other two towers, internal communication was by means of a staircase within the central pillar.[4]

The armament varied considerably between the three towers. When first built the Prince of Wales Tower mounted two 24pdr guns and four 68pdr carronades on the gun platform firing through embrasures, and four 6pdr guns were mounted within the tower on the first floor. By

1811, when the roof was so rotten that it could no longer support the weight of even a reduced number of guns, a decision was taken to disarm the tower temporarily. Board of Ordnance approval was received to rebuild the tower by constructing a brick bomb-proof arch to support the gun platform and thus protect the tower from plunging fire from both mortars and howitzers. This alteration necessitated the removal of the hollow central pillar and so access to each floor inside the tower was simply by ladder through a trapdoor in the gun platform and the first floor. The embrasures in the parapet were also closed up and the armament was mounted *en barbette*, that is, firing over the parapet rather than through embrasures. The closure of the embrasures meant that the mode of entrance to the tower had to be changed so that it was through a door at ground level which had been opened in the wall when a new magazine was built about 1805. When the alterations were complete in 1812 the armament of the tower was changed to two 24pdr guns and four 24pdr carronades, and the tower came to resemble more closely a very large Martello tower.

Since the role of the Clarence and the York Tower was to act as keeps for the defence of the redoubts from infantry attack, there was less incentive to rebuild them, as had been done with the Prince of Wales Tower, which stood alone and was not sited within a redoubt. Some modifications were carried out to the Clarence Tower, including the building of a magazine for a hundred barrels of gunpowder on the ground floor inside the tower and the closing up of the parapet embrasures on the landward side to provide additional protection for the men manning the guns. At the same time the height of the parapet on the seaward side was reduced to 3ft (0.9m).

The Prince of Wales Tower at Halifax; the photograph shows the tower in 1882. [PRO WO 78/4644]

The wooden roofs of the two towers were replaced but not rebuilt and this ensured that the armament had to be limited to lighter weapons. In 1808 the Duke of Clarence Tower had four 32pdr carronades and four 24pdr carronades on top and four obsolescent 8in brass howitzers inside on the first floor, the latter firing through embrasures. By 1812 the howitzers had been removed and replaced by four additional 24pdr carronades. On the gun platform the armament was changed to eight 24pdr carronades on traversing slides. The Duke of York Tower was the most lightly armed of the three towers and in 1810 had six 12pdr carronades on the gun platform and two 6pdr guns inside the tower.[5]

The importance of Halifax to the British grew with its development as a major convoy-assembly point and as a base for the Royal Navy. The threat to the city, however, came not just from the French but increasingly from the United States as a result of American anger at the Royal Navy's 'stop and search' policy towards their ships. Because of this latter and obviously greater threat, the British authorities decided to improve the defences of the harbour. Between 1794 and 1800 the Duke of Kent had constructed a 'star' fort, known as Fort Charlotte, on George's Island, with a wooden blockhouse in the centre. The fort was poorly sited on the island and the blockhouse too small to accommodate the garrison, so in 1805 Captain William Fenwick, RE, the Commanding Engineer, suggested that the blockhouse should be replaced by a strong masonry tower to act as an effective keep. The Anglo-American crisis of 1807-08 brought the matter of improving the George's Island defences to the fore and in 1810 the Committee of Engineers in England recommended the erection of a stone tower to replace the blockhouse and act as a magazine.[6]

The tower was not completed until 1812 and, when it had been, it was more like an English Martello tower than the three earlier Halifax structures. It had a diameter of 43ft (13.2m) but the height is unknown. The tower had two storeys and the masonry gun platform was built on a bomb-proof arch and the whole was supported by a solid central pillar 5ft (1.53m) thick. Since the tower acted as a keep for the fort, the armament was once again carronades with four 24pdrs on the gun platform and four 12pdrs inside the tower firing through embrasures. As in the English Martello towers, the George's Island Tower had a staircase built within the 7ft (2.15m) thick wall and a magazine on the ground floor; but unlike those towers it was loopholed for musketry on both floors.

Work on the final tower at Halifax, the Sherbrooke Tower, was started in 1814. Named after Lieutenant-General Sir John

Sherbrooke, the Lieutenant Governor of Nova Scotia, the tower was to be sited on Maugher Beach, a shingle beach on McNab Island. Sherbrooke believed the tower would support York Redoubt by engaging ships which could not be engaged by that redoubt and it was planned as a two-storey, circular Martello tower for four heavy guns which were to be mounted *en barbette* on the gun platform. As with the others, this tower was originally authorized to be built as a 'field work' but construction was slow as a result of difficulties in obtaining materials and a change in design from rubble masonry to ashlar. By 1816 the wall of the tower was only 8ft (2.4m) high when, as a result of the end of the Napoleonic Wars in Europe, orders came to stop all work on field defences. The partially completed tower was placed in a state of care and maintenance in the hope that its completion would eventually be authorized, but this did not occur until 1828 when the

The Sherbrooke Tower, Halifax, showing its design when it was completed as a lighthouse. [PRO MPH 495]

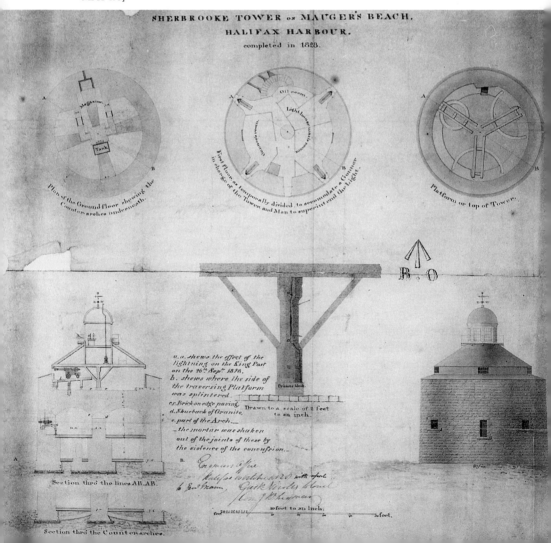

decision was taken to complete it as a combined Martello tower and lighthouse.[7]

The use of the tower as a lighthouse presented the post-1815 engineers with something of a problem when deciding how to incorporate the armament. This was eventually solved by raising the light on a platform over the guns on the platform and supporting the light on a central king post. This reduced the armament on the top of the tower from the four heavy guns originally planned to two, each with a limited traverse, while below, on the first floor, there were four carronades firing through embrasures.

Deteriorating Anglo-American relations in the period 1807-12, which had led to the construction of the two later towers at Halifax, also resulted in a review of the fortifications of Quebec. A proposal that resulted from this was to defend the Plains of Abraham with detached field works to prevent an enemy from launching a regular siege and bombardment from the Plains. The proposal resulted in a lengthy debate between the Inspector General of Fortifications and the Master General of the Ordnance on the merits of towers other than for coast defence. The Inspector General was against the proposal, but the Master General supported it. Major-General Mann proposed the construction of an entrenched camp but the new Governor General of British North America, Lieutenant-General Sir James Craig, rejected this proposal as requiring a large garrison which was unlikely ever to be available. In 1808 in a report to Viscount Castlereagh, Craig wrote:

> '*indeed the occupying these* [the Heights of Abraham] *at the least expence* [sic] *of men has been the principal object with us - and it is upon that principle as well as the consideration of their requiring the least time in their construction that we have determined on a range of towers.*'[8]

General Craig, growing impatient at the delay in obtaining a decision and fearful of an American invasion, took the matter into his own hands and gave instructions that work on the towers should be started, once again under the heading of 'field works'. Sir James Craig had considerable experience of the value of towers as a cheap and effective form of defence. He had previously served as Lieutenant Governor of Jersey and knew the towers on that island, and when commanding the British forces at the Cape of Good Hope in 1796 he had ordered the construction of two there. Before being sent to Canada as Governor General he had commanded in the south of England and so it is perhaps understandable that the design used for the Quebec towers was that used for the towers of Kent and Sussex.[9]

Towers 2 and 3, the largest, were 56ft (17.2m) in diameter and 33ft (10.15m) high, while Towers 1 and 4 were slightly smaller. Each of the two large ones had two embrasures for guns or carronades at first-floor level and could mount up to five guns of assorted calibres on the gun platform. Tower 2 mounted five guns on the gun platform in addition to two 9pdr guns on the first floor, while Tower 3, although designed to mount five guns on top, only ever received three, two 24pdr guns mounted *en barbette* and one 68pdr carronade firing through an embrasure. Towers 1 and 4, the two smaller towers, mounted only one gun on the gun platform, Tower 1 having one 24pdr gun on a traversing platform and Tower 4 one 18pdr, also on a traversing platform.

All the towers were constructed of sandstone ashlar and were unusual in having one section of the parapet, that over the doorway and on the side away from an approaching enemy, about 2ft (0.6m) lower than the rest of the parapet, and in Tower 4 there was an additional gallery within the main parapet extending almost halfway round the tower. This gallery was designed to enable riflemen to fire towards the north and the east without interrupting the working of the single gun on the platform. In 1823 cedar shingle roofs were added to protect the towers and guns from the severe weather. As in the English towers, those at Quebec had cisterns in the basement together with a powder magazine capable of holding 75 barrels in Towers 1 and 4, and 150 barrels in Towers 2 and 3.

The last tower of this period was built at Saint John, the main port of New Brunswick. This port, although not as strategically important

Tower No.1 at Quebec; it is shown here after recent refurbishment and with a replacement shingle roof similar to the original one of 1825. [Author's collection]

The Carleton Tower, Saint John, New Brunswick. [Author's collection]

as Halifax, was still significant as a commercial centre and minor naval base. Protected against raids by a number of batteries, the harbour was, nevertheless, vulnerable to an attack by land from the west and the decision was taken to build a stone tower and four redoubts on heights to the rear of Carleton, a small town on the western shore of the harbour opposite Saint John. Construction of the Carleton Tower started in 1813 and the design of the tower was that of a standard English south-coast tower built of rubble masonry with a batter to the wall. The tower was 50ft (15.4m) in diameter and 30ft (9.25m) high. The thick, bomb-proof arch supporting the roof and the gun platform was itself supported by a masonry pillar, but this had a narrow chute running up its centre suitable for raising ammunition. The tower was designed to mount two 24pdr carronades on the platform and three 4pdr guns on the first floor; but by the end of the war with the United States in 1815 no guns had been mounted on the tower nor was the line of redoubts ever built. The Carleton Tower was left to stand alone, a solitary defence work bereft of any tactical value.[10]

Subsequently in 1865 the Carleton Tower did regain a fleeting moment of military importance. The Fenian Brotherhood planned a series of attacks on Canada from the United States, and New Brunswick appeared particularly vulnerable because of its long border with Maine. The Carleton Tower was again pressed into service as part of a line of defences to protect Saint John from attack from the west. Repairs to the tower were carried out but no guns were available to mount on the tower until after the Fenian threat had disappeared in 1866. Two 32pdr guns were eventually mounted but, in the long tradition of Martello towers, the Carleton Tower was ready for action only when there was no longer a threat.[11]

In 1923 the Carleton Tower was declared a national historic site but during the Second World War it was taken back into use by the Canadian Army, first as an air observation post and then in 1941 it became the Saint John Fire Command Post. For this role a new, two-storey, concrete superstructure was built on the original gun platform to house the position-finding and communication equipment, enabling the new fire command post to control the fire of the four batteries defending Saint John.

The later history of the Canadian towers was of their use as barrack accommodation until the British forces withdrew from Canada in 1870-71, when the majority of the towers were handed over to the Dominion government. Only in Halifax did British troops remain after 1870 to protect the naval base, and the Prince of Wales, the Clarence and the York Tower continued to be maintained as part of the defences of the base. In 1862 the ground floor of the Prince of Wales Tower was converted into a large powder magazine and an armament of four 32pdr guns was retained on the gun platform, while four machicolations were added to the parapet. A proposal to protect the tower with a redoubt was never implemented and the tower remained, a highly vulnerable magazine sited in an exposed position, until the final withdrawal of British troops in 1906. The Clarence Tower was reconstructed in 1867 as part of a remodelled and more powerful Fort Clarence and reduced in height, and further reduced in 1889, by which date only the ground-floor magazine remained. The George's Island tower was demolished in 1877 and in the 1890s the upper floors of the York Tower were gutted by fire, but the Sherbrooke Tower continued in use as a lighthouse for many years.

Today only five of these Canadian towers remain. The Prince of Wales Tower is now part of the Halifax Defence Complex and is a museum, and the Carleton Tower at Saint John has also been refurbished and opened as a museum by Parks Canada. Towers 1, 2 and 4 at Quebec remain, Tower 3 having been demolished in 1905. The other towers were restored in 1937 and Tower 4 was used as an observatory by the Royal Astronomical Society of Canada between 1941 and 1962. The three towers are now maintained by the National Battlefields Commission and are open to the public.

These towers were not the only Martello towers to be built in Canada. A further four large towers and two small ones were built at Kingston, Ontario, between 1845 and 1848. These towers will be described in Chapter 9.

CHAPTER 8

The Defence of Empire

The Mediterranean

The defence of Britain from invasion, the maintenance of British rule in India, and the wealth generated as a result of controlling India's trade, depended on the Royal Navy's command of the seas. This in turn depended upon the Royal Navy having bases and secure anchorages from which to operate throughout the world. Protection of these bases was essential and, as in Britain, the commanders overseas turned to gun-towers to provide a quick and effective solution to this problem.

As we have seen, towers had been built on Minorca between 1798 and 1802 when the island was the principal base for the Navy in the Mediterranean. With the loss of Minorca the British were forced to look to the Kingdom of Naples to provide a new base and by 1810 the British were operating from Sicily - a bankrupt kingdom supported by British gold, ships and between ten and fifteen thousand British troops. Because an effective blockade of the French Mediterranean ports was difficult, if not almost impossible, due to the unfavourable prevailing winds, the British commander in Sicily in 1810, Major-General Lord William Bentinck, could not dismiss the possibility that the French might attempt to land troops on the island. These might be shipped direct from France or, more likely, from Calabria where Marshal Murat, Napoleon's puppet King of Naples, had assembled an invasion force and boats ready to cross the strait to Messina. This force was kept at bay by ships of the Royal Navy and a flotilla of Anglo-Sicilian gunboats, but the strait was so narrow that there was a real danger that a substantial number of French troops might be ferried across before British ships could intervene, particularly if the wind was against the British.

To deter the French from invading the island British troops supported the Sicilian army and British garrisons were stationed in Messina, Milazzo and the two southern ports of Syracuse and Augusta, the latter two at the insistence of the Commander-in-Chief of the Mediterranean Fleet, Admiral Lord Collingwood. Existing fortifications at Messina, Milazzo and Augusta were repaired and improved and the decision was taken to fortify the coastline between

Messina and the headland of Faro, the closest point on the island to the Italian mainland.

Much of the work was carried out under the direction of the British commanding Engineer of the Anglo-Sicilian forces, Colonel Alexander Bryce, RE, and in receipts provided by the Sicilian engineer officer Captain Francisco Ferrara in 1815 for fortifications handed over by the British, two towers are mentioned which were built to defend Milazzo and five more as part of the Faro Lines. Construction of these towers was suggested as early as 1799 when Lieutenant-General Sir Charles Stuart was sent to inspect the defences of Sicily. Stuart had ordered the building of the Minorcan towers the previous year so that it is not surprising to find his recommendation in a report to Sir William Hamilton, the British ambassador in Naples, that a number of bomb-proof round towers, each for a garrison of thirty men should be built, one at Messina, 'two on the extreme Heights commanding the Road from Milazzo, one at the Grotta, another at the Faro, and one of four times the Capacity upon the opposite Coast.'[1]

The two towers at Milazzo were converted from older, square towers which stood on the promontory and, together with a line of entrenchments, defended the approach to the town from the sea. The improved towers were described by the Sicilian engineer as having a circular stone parapet and they mounted a single 'coastal gun', probably a 24pdr, on a centrally-mounted, traversing carriage. These two towers were named Cole's Tower and Paget's Tower by the British and each was of two storeys with a magazine and cistern on the ground floor with entry at first-floor level by means of a removable wooden ladder.[2]

The most extensive system of field works and permanent fortifications was built between Messina and the lighthouse tower at the point of Faro, a distance of some 9 miles (14.4 km) by road, and also in the mountains immediately behind the coast road. The aim was to prevent the French from landing on the flat headland at Faro and then advancing along the road to Messina. A total of fourteen new, open batteries with guns mounted *en barbette* were built along the coast together with three redoubts and five towers, all to supplement the existing Pelorus Tower at Faro and two older redoubts. Additional batteries and gun positions were also constructed to defend a series of new military roads built inland across the mountains. Much of this work was planned under the direction of Colonel Bryce.

The Faro Lines were completed by 1815, including the five towers, two between the villages of St. Agata and Ganzirri, one between

Ganzirri and Faro and two on the promontory itself. All five towers were built to a basic design and were circular, with two storeys and with the main gun platform on top of the towers. The gun platform was built above a bomb-proof arch which, in turn, was supported by a strong, central column similar to those in the English Martello towers. They were armed with a single 24pdr gun on the platform and three 24pdr carronades, two firing through embrasures on the first floor. Entrance to the towers was by means of a rope ladder through one of the embrasures; but inside the tower access to the ground floor and the gun platform was by means of a staircase built into the wall of the tower. Four of the towers had fresh water cisterns on the ground floor and the Mazzone tower on the headland had a well.[3]

The two towers at St. Agata and Ganzirri both supported newly constructed, permanent fortifications. The tower at St. Agata was an older one which stood on a small hill supporting a new redoubt for

Section and plan of the tower built about 1810 on the isthmus of Magnisi in the Bay of Augusta, Sicily. [Austrian State Archives]

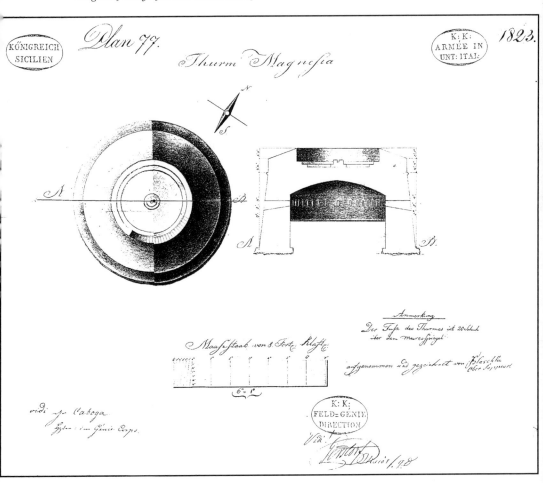

five 24pdr guns. It was rebuilt as a Martello tower in 1811 together
with the new Ganzirri tower which stood on level ground to the rear
of the village of the same name which also supported a permanent
redoubt. About 1½ miles (2.4 km) to the east of Ganzirri stood the
third tower in the rear of a line of trenches 350yd (323m) long which
extended from the beach to the edge of one of the two lakes on the
promontory. These lakes, which were known to the British as Long
Lake and Round Lake, were also included in the overall defensive plan
by the construction of the Mazzone Canal linking the lakes and the
sea and so providing an effective defensive water barrier across the
promontory while also providing a safe anchorage for the flotilla of
Anglo-Sicilian gunboats.

One tower, sometimes called the Cariddi Tower, was built close to
the beach to defend the entrance to the new canal which led into
Round Lake from the south. The fourth tower, the Mazzone Tower,
was also built close to the beach but this tower defended the narrow
neck of land between Round Lake and the sea to the north and the
northern entrance to the lake. This latter tower was a typical Martello
tower and is the only one of these still in existence today, being
currently used as a base to support radio and television antennas. The
two towers at Faro are marked as Martello towers on a chart of the
Strait of Messina made by Captain Henry Smith, RN in 1823, and are
so described in the 'Memoir' which accompanied his atlas of Sicily.

Between Catania and Syracuse in the Bay of Augusta there was a
further Martello tower on the highest point of the island of Magnisi.
This small island is linked to the mainland by a causeway at low tide
and the tower, which was described by Smith as 'a stout Martello
tower', commanded the whole island, including the two small bays,
and was obviously situated to deter an enemy landing on the coast
south of Augusta.

The Magnisi tower was circular in shape and its dimensions were
similar to those of the standard English south-coast tower, having a
diameter of 45ft (13.8m) and a height of 32ft (9.8m). It was built of
brick with a central pillar supporting a bomb-proof arch and the base
of the parapet was marked externally by a stone string-course or
cordon. Inside the tower the gun platform and the first floor were
linked by a stone staircase built within the thickness of the wall of the
tower which varied between 8ft 6in (2.6m) and 7ft 4in (2.25m). A
single heavy gun on a traversing platform was mounted on the gun
platform, but at the ground- and the first-floor level there was a line
of loopholes running all round the tower. On the ground floor were
the magazine, storeroom and cistern; access to these was gained by

means of two trapdoors and ladders from the first floor.

On the first-floor level there was the usual door and two windows, and the tower was protected on the landward side by a glacis, but unusually this was built up against the wall of the tower. Smith described the glacis as being 'injudicially attached... for a space between them [the door and the glacis], and entrance by a draw-bridge, would have rendered the whole more secure.'[4] Despite the heavy industrialization which today has spread along the shores of the Bay of Augusta, the tower remains in reasonable condition and is still the only structure on the island.

In 1811 Captain William Hoste, RN, the victor of the Battle of Lissa against a force of French and Venetian frigates, immediately recognized the strategic value of Lissa as an advanced naval base and dockyard vital for control of the Adriatic. In a report to the Rt Hon. Charles Yorke, the First Lord of the Admiralty, he wrote recommending that the island should be fortified as a British base. In a letter dated 22 August 1811 he wrote:

> *'I think a Martello Tower built on the emminence* [sic] *at the head of the harbour to secure it from a "Coup de Main" with a Garrison of 3 or 400 men would, whilst you possess a naval superiority, keep it quite secure from any attack from the opposite coast of Dalmatia or Apulia.'*[5]

Naval officers were very conscious of the efficacy of towers as defensive coastal fortifications and Hoste and his superior officer Admiral Fremantle were well aware of the rough handling Sir Sydney Smith's ship HMS *Pompee* (80 guns) had received in 1806 when it engaged an Italian coastal tower at Licosa in the Gulf of Naples. Hoste may also have been influenced by his brother George, a captain in the Royal Engineers serving in Sicily, who was probably responsible for the tower at Augusta. The report, or possibly one from Captain Sir Charles Rowley, RN who succeeded Hoste in the Adriatic and who made similar recommendations regarding Lissa, reached Lord Liverpool, the Secretary for War, probably from the Admiralty. In August 1811 Liverpool wrote to Lord William Bentinck concerning the occupation of Lissa:

> *'I feel it advisable to recommend this Measure to Your Lordship's early attention, provided you find the works which may be requisite for the defence of the Island, and particularly of the Harbour, are not likely to be attended with a serious Expence* [sic], *or to require any considerable body of regular troops for their protection.'*[6]

The following year Bentinck despatched a small force under the command of Lieutenant-Colonel George Robertson to secure the island.

Before the occupation Captain William Bennett, RE had been sent to Lissa to 'Inspect into the kinds of defence necessary for its protection should it be found desirable to be possessed by the British Government',[7] for even before the Battle of Lissa the island had been used as the main British base in the Adriatic. However, Captain John Henryson, RE was ordered to accompany the expedition because Bennett's report had proved lacking in the detail required by the authorities in Sicily. His first task was to supervise the construction of fortifications, including a citadel and three Martello towers to defend the town and harbour of Porto San Giorgio. By March 1813 the citadel and two towers had been completed but work on the third was stopped when it was half completed because of increasing cost.[8]

The citadel, Fort George, was built on a low headland controlling the entrance to the harbour and was a substantial rectangular fort with two courtyards, one containing officers' quarters, barracks and the magazines, and a second which contained a vast cistern for rainwater and the main battery. The three Martello towers were built in a semi-circle on the hills behind the town of Porto San Giorgio and their primary function was to defend the harbour. The Bentinck Tower was sited to the rear of Fort George to secure high ground which dominated the fort, while the Robertson Tower, a slightly larger one, was built on a hill inland and south of the town. The third tower, Fort Wellington, was built on the headland opposite Fort George, 585ft (180m) above sea level.

All three towers had a diameter of between 40 and 43ft (12.3 to 13.2m) and a height of 32ft (9.8m). They were designed to mount a single gun on a traversing platform, probably a 24pdr, on the gun platform, and in all three towers this was constructed over a bomb-proof arch supported by a central pillar. The towers were circular with near-vertical walls without machicolation, and the Robertson Tower, unlike the Bentinck Tower, had an entrance at ground level. In the Robertson Tower there was a line of loopholes on the first floor with a line of smaller

Ruins of Fort Wellington, Lissa (Vis); the tower was badly damaged by bombardment when the Italian fleet attacked the island in 1866. [Author's photograph]

loopholes, or possibly ventilation apertures, in the ground-floor wall. From their dominating positions, the towers in conjunction with Fort George controlled not only the entrance to the harbour but also the town of Porto San Giorgio itself.

The fortifications on the island were, however, controlled by the British for only a short time before they handed over the island to Austria in 1815. Some years later the Austrians constructed two more modern batteries to supplement the older defences and one of these batteries was sited in front of the Bentinck Tower. Fort George and the three towers were partly destroyed in a bombardment during the second Battle of Lissa in 1866 between the Austrian and the Italian fleet, but Fort George, which was repaired by the Austrians after the battle, and the remains of Fort Wellington and Bentinck Tower may still be seen today. Robertson Tower, however, has disappeared.

Plan and section of Fort Wellington on the island of Curzola (Korcula). [Austrian State Archives]

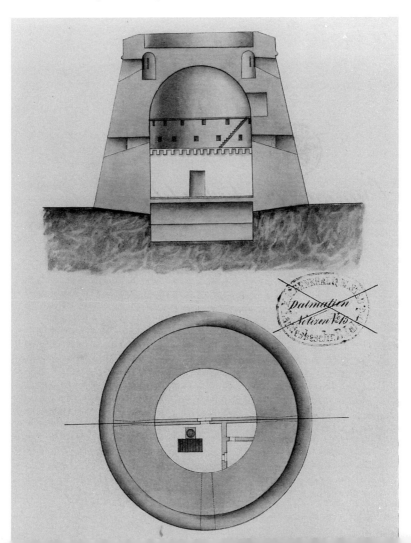

In February 1813 the decision was taken to capture the island of
Curzola (Korcula) to enable it to be used as a base from which to inter-
cept the coasting trade by means of which the French garrisons on the
Dalmatian coast were supplied. Troops from Lissa, again under the
command of Colonel Robertson, captured the island after only slight
opposition from the French, and Captain Pearce Lowen, a British
officer serving with the Royal Corsican Rangers, remained in
command of the garrison.[9] Lowen was responsible for the adminis-
tration of the newly-captured island and he ordered the construction
of a tower, also named Fort Wellington, on a hill overlooking the town
and the harbour on the site of the seventeenth-century Fort St. Blaise
built by the Venetians. Work on the tower was completed in August
1813 but the design differed in a number of respects from that of a
standard Martello tower.

   Fort Wellington was a circular, two-storey tower, constructed

Fort Wellington, Curzola (Korcula), as it is today. [Author's photograph]

without a central pillar and with a firing gallery built into the bomb-proof section of the roof below the parapet. The wall of the tower had a steep batter with a line of musketry loopholes for the firing gallery immediately below the level of the parapet, and a double line of alternating loopholes at first-floor level. The magazine and the store were on the ground floor and smaller ventilation slits were provided at this level. Entrance to the tower was by means of a removable ladder through a doorway and entrance passage which was sited 6ft (1.85m) above the level of the first floor; this necessitated the use of a second ladder inside the tower, a feature also found in the smaller British towers on Minorca.[10] A short, internal staircase led from the side wall of the entrance passage to the upper firing gallery and the roof platform. There was no provision for a gun to be mounted on the tower and it would seem that it was designed as a musketry tower to defend the old fort against infantry attack.

This design seems more akin to earlier Venetian towers and bastions found elsewhere on the Adriatic coasts of Italy and Dalmatia and probably resulted from the fact that the tower was designed and built under the supervision of an infantry officer. Since Captain Henryson had left Lissa by April 1813, the tower reflected the experience of the British commander on the island, Captain Pearce Lowen, and the local builders and stonemasons. The tower saw action briefly in the Second World War when it was captured from its Italian garrison by Yugoslav partisans in 1943. The tower still stands today in good condition, to support telecommunication equipment, and is an interesting relic of British military architecture in the Adriatic.

The Route to India

Before the opening of the Suez Canal in the later part of the nineteenth century, the key to the sea route to India was not the Mediterranean but the Cape of Good Hope. Cape Colony and Cape Town had been captured from the Dutch in 1795 and it was at Cape Town that two towers were built in 1796, on the orders of Major-General James Craig, by Captain George Bridges, RE who was transferred three years later from Cape Town to Minorca. The two Cape towers, Craig's Tower and the tower at Simon's Town, were sited one immediately to the north of Cape Town to guard the coast and the road to Wynberg and the other to defend Simon's Town Bay. Both were erected as keeps for adjacent batteries. It has been said that these were not Martello towers and certainly in design they were different both from Martello towers and from each other in a number of important ways. Nevertheless, like the three towers built about the same time at Halifax, the two Cape towers were undoubtedly forerunners of the Martello towers and their design served to influence a number of engineer officers who were later to be involved in the construction of the Martello towers.

Both towers were about 27ft (8.3m) high with a diameter of 46ft (14.15m) for the Simon's Town tower and 40ft (12.3m) for Craig's Tower. The main difference between the two was that the tower at Simon's Town was circular but Craig's Tower was D-shaped, with a single line of musketry embrasures along the straight section of the wall at first-floor level. The Simon's Town tower had a doorway at ground level and three large embrasures, probably originally designed for carronades, opening on the land side and covering the approach to the battery from the rear. Both towers had a machicolation made of wood over the doorway and Craig's Tower had three embrasures in the straight section of the parapet, with the central embrasure acting

Simon's Town Tower, Cape Town, South Africa. [Simon's Town Museum]

as an entrance to the machicolation which was clearly added at a later date, after the tower had been completed. To the right of the machicolation, in the curved section of the wall, there was a fourth, larger embrasure covering an arc from 90 to 120 degrees. The walls of both towers had no batter and were 6ft (1.8m) thick, except that of the straight section of the wall of Craig's Tower which was only half that thickness.[11]

Neither tower had a bomb-proof roof and only Craig's Tower was ever armed, when between 1812 and 1818, and perhaps for some years after, a single brass 6pdr gun, taken when the Cape of Good Hope was captured from the Dutch, was shown as the armament in the Ordnance returns of that period.[12] There is no record of any guns being mounted on or in the tower at Simon's Town which was used primarily as a magazine for the battery. Craig's Tower was demolished in the late nineteenth century but that at Simon's Town continued in military use until the beginning of this century and was from then until recently used as a museum. It now stands unused within the perimeter of the naval base.

The two Cape Colony towers probably influenced the design of another tower built the following year, 1797, on the island of St. Helena in the South Atlantic. By the end of the eighteenth century this small volcanic island, situated some 1,000 miles (1,600 kilometres) off the western coast of Africa and double that distance from Cape Town, had become an important staging post for ships sailing round the Cape of Good Hope to India. The island, which had been British since 1661, was garrisoned and fortified by troops of the East India Company.

Ladder Hill, one side of the steep valley in which the little capital of Jamestown is situated, was fortified in 1797 by Governor Brooke. He ordered a battery of two 18pdr guns to be built on the top of the hill sited to fire seaward, with a rubble masonry tower mounting two 12 pdr guns to defend the approaches to the battery from the rear. The tower was very similar in design to the tower at Simon's Town, being a simple circular tower with a diameter of about 45ft (13.8m) and a height of approximately 20ft (6.15m), finally being incorporated into the new High Knoll Fort built in 1895.

There was a third tower in Africa, built on Tower Hill in Freetown in Sierra Leone, by the Sierra Leone Company before it became a Crown Colony in 1808. In 1794 a defenceless Freetown was destroyed by a French naval squadron and in 1800 an unsuccessful uprising of the original settlers from Nova Scotia, who feared the arrival of additional black settlers, had caused the Company to consider seriously withdrawing from Sierra Leone. After considerable debate the directors took the decision to remain and the British government granted the Company £7,000, with the promise of a further £8,000 to follow, for the construction of a fort, later known as Fort Thornton.[13] In 1802, in the Sierra Leone Company's petition to Parliament, the point was made that Fort Thornton was commanded by an adjacent hill which would make the fort difficult to hold against a European enemy equipped with artillery and in 1804 a decision was taken to erect a tower on the hill. The Board of Ordnance was requested 'To furnish the Court of Directors with the model of the tower which is at present the most approved', and the foundation stone was laid in 1805.[14] By 1807 the Company was reporting that 'A strong Martello tower had been erected which was to be called "Union Tower"'. The name of the hill was changed, with amazing lack of originality, from Wansey Hill to Tower Hill.

It was intended that three towers should be constructed to defend Freetown, but in the end only Union Tower was completed. The tower was to mount 'One or two heavy pieces of cannon', but by 1808 the first Governor of the new colony found 'That the Martello tower on the hill, the only good work in the place, was of no use for want of a gun', and by 1827 the tower had been partially demolished. In 1845 Major Rowley, of the West India Regiment, commanding the garrison, suggested the conversion of the remains of the tower into a small military prison. In a letter to the Board of Ordnance he wrote: 'There is an old Martello tower, conveniently situated in the barrack enclosure

The tower at La Preneuse, Black River Bay, Mauritius. [Author's collection]

now rather dilapidated in consequence of efforts made to pull it down which owing to the strength and solidity of the masonry has not been effected.'[15] The tower had a diameter of 43ft (12.25m) but by 1845 the wall stood only 17ft (5.25m) high.

However, it is nearer to India on a small island in the middle of the Indian Ocean where today may be found some of the best examples of Martello towers outside the United Kingdom. Mauritius was captured from the French in 1810 and was retained by the British after 1815. As an ex-French possession and still retaining a large number of French settlers as part of the population, the British Governor was concerned not only with the defence of the island from any external threat but also with maintaining internal security. With the end of the Napoleonic Wars the existing defences of the island were allowed to fall into disrepair, since economies in defence spending meant that no money was available for a remote dependency such as Mauritius. However, by 1825 the Governor, Sir Lowry Cole, became concerned at the poor state of the defences and instructed the senior artillery and engineer officers on the island, Lieutenant-Colonel Brough, RA and Lieutenant-Colonel Buchanan, RE, to carry out a review of the existing defence works. The recommendations made in their report included the construction of a citadel at Port Louis and the construction or improvement of a number of coastal batteries and towers at Port Louis, Grand River North West, Black River Bay, Mahebourg and Tombeau Bay. These plans were approved by the Governor and submitted to the Board of Ordnance three years later in August 1828.[16]

This leisurely consideration of improvements to the island's defences might have stopped on the desk of the Master General of the Ordnance had it not been that the bill for the abolition of slavery was at that time coming before Parliament. Despite the fact that financial compensation was to be offered, it was quite clear that the French plantation owners on Mauritius would be particularly badly affected by the freeing of their slaves. The British authorities became concerned at the possibility of an insurrection on the island fomented by the pro-French settlers and slave owners and supported by the French from their nearby base on Réunion. So, in 1829, the Board of Ordnance rapidly authorized the immediate construction of the citadel at Port Louis, to be called Fort Adelaide, and five Martello towers. One tower, named Cunningham Tower after Lieutenant-Colonel Cunningham, the commanding Royal Engineer, was constructed as part of Fort George on Ile au Tonneliers on the outskirts of Port Louis; two towers were built at Grand River North

West and two more were built to support existing batteries, which were also impoved, at the mouth of the Black River. Construction was given further impetus by the despatch of a French naval squadron to the Indian Ocean in 1831, and the Board of Ordnance sent additional Royal Engineers to build the new defences and the necessary guns to arm them. As a result all the towers were complete by 1834.

It would appear from 'A Statement of Barrack Buildings in Mauritius', dated 1838, that all five Martello towers were built to a standard, circular design.[17] The height is given as 39ft (12m), although Cunningham Tower is shown in a plan and section dated 1833 as being only 35ft (10.7m) high and the La Preneuse tower at the mouth of the Black River was shown on a plan of the same date as being 30ft (9.2m) high.[18] The external diameter of all the towers was given as 43ft (13.2m). There is a disparity between the dimensions given in the 1838 'Statement' and the dimensions as they exist today, which are actually less, being 30ft (9.2m) in height and 32ft (9.8m) in diameter.

All the towers were constructed of black basalt blocks and, like the English south-coast towers, the wall facing the sea was almost double in thickness that of the rear wall. The thickness at the front of the Black River and the Grand River North West tower was 11ft (3.38m) at the

Hambantota Tower, Sri Lanka: this clearly shows the overhanging parapet wall. [Author's collection]

front and 6ft (1.8m) at the rear. The towers were built on two levels with a magazine for thirty barrels of gunpowder on the ground floor together with a cistern holding 4,500 gallons of fresh water. The living accommodation for the garrison of one officer and fifteen soldiers was on the first floor and it was at this level that the tower was entered through a doorway approached up a removable ladder. Unlike the English towers, there was only one window and one vertical firing slit in the wall of the Black River and the Grand River North West tower, but the now-demolished Cunningham Tower differed from the others in having two windows and a number of small apertures for the ventilation of the magazine at ground-floor level.[19] The armament of the towers, except Cunningham Tower, was one 24pdr gun and one $5^1/_2$in howitzer each. Cunningham Tower, acting as a keep for Fort George, was armed with three 24pdr carronades.

Only three of the five towers remain. Cunningham Tower has been demolished together with the tower on the southern side of Grand River North West. Of the others, the tower at La Preneuse, in Black River Bay, has been refurbished by the Friends of the Environment in Mauritius and is open to the public, while the second tower at the entrance to the Black River, at Pointe de L'Harmonie, has been taken into the care of the Ministry of Arts and Culture and it is hoped will also be preserved.

Another tower on the route to India, and much closer to the sub-continent, was built at Hambantota, a small port on the most southerly coast of Ceylon (now Sri Lanka). It would appear that the tower was built between 1804 and 1806 after Ceylon had been ceded to Britain by the Dutch under the Treaty of Amiens in 1802. The tower was built to protect the small harbour and settlement of Hambantota after an unsuccessful attack by insurgent Kandian forces in 1803. Cordiner in his book *A Description of Ceylon,* which records visits to Hambantota in 1801 and 1803, does not mention a tower, but Sir Alexander Johnston said in an account of his travels, when he visited in 1806: 'I went over the tower built by Captain Goper of the Engineers'. Goper is an elusive individual whose name does not appear in the Army Lists of the time. There was a Captain Alexander Cowper of the Bombay Engineers serving in 1806 but there is no indication that he was serving in Ceylon at that date and was the officer referred to by Johnston. However, the commanding engineer in Ceylon at the time of the tower's construction was Captain Bridges, the same Captain Bridges who was involved in the design of the Simon's Town tower at the Cape of Good Hope in 1796, which the tower at Hambantota resembles.

Like the Simon's Town tower, the tower at Hambantota had a
vertical wall but there was an unusual projecting rim around the
parapet. The height of the tower was similar to that of the Simon's
Town tower, being 25ft (7.6m) high, but the base diameter was smaller
at 40ft (12m). Like the English towers, entrance was through a
doorway on the first floor, but unlike them, the Hambantota tower had
a number of large loopholes. On the ground floor there was a storeroom and a magazine with a capacity of forty barrels of gunpowder.

The recorded armament of the tower consisted mainly of small
guns, including two iron 6pdr guns, two iron and one brass 3pdr guns
and a number of 2pdr and 1pdr guns. However, by 1813 one 5$^{1}/_{2}$in
howitzer had replaced some of the smaller guns and in 1814 two 18pdr
carronades were added. The only carriages shown in the Ordnance
returns of this period were travelling carrriages until 1813 when the
5$^{1}/_{2}$in howitzer was shown as having a wooden 'howitzer' carriage. So
it would seem probable that at this date the tower was used primarily
for the storage of field ordnance, but the howitzer was provided for
the defence of the tower itself.[20]

Finally, in India itself seven towers were built as part of the defences
of Shahjahanabad, the old walled city of Delhi built by the Emperor
Shah Jahan between 1638 and 1649. The city was captured by the
British under General Lord Lake in 1803 during the Second Mahratta
War, but the following year the British were themselves besieged in
Delhi by the Mahratta forces. The fight for the city was all the more
gallant since 'The only defence the City had was an old wall, of the

*One of the seven towers built by the British to reinforce the defences of Old Delhi
(Shahjahanabad).* [Author's photograph]

worst description of masonry, sufficiently high, but in many places without a parapet, nowhere fit for mounting a gun upon, or able to stand the shock of one fired.'[21]

With the final defeat of the Mahrattas in 1805-06 the British were slow in improving the defences of the city and repairing the old wall which had a circumference of some 7 miles (11 km), and it was not until 1814 that Sir Charles Metcalfe, then the Resident at Delhi, sought permission for the repair and modernization of the defences. Sir Charles believed that the wall should be rebuilt with stone rather than mud but it was not until ten years later that this work was carried out. In 1824 Reginald Heber, Bishop of Calcutta and author of many well-known hymns, in his *Narrative of a Journey through the Upper Province of India* described Delhi as being 'surrounded by an embattled wall, which the English Government have put into repair and are now engaged in strengthening with bastions, a moat, and a regular glacis', together with the seven Martello towers interspersed between the bastions.

To the purist, the Delhi towers might appear to be detached circular bastions but to a senior Royal Engineers officer present at the siege they were undoubtedly Martello towers. To Colonel Richard Baird Smith, RE the fortifications of the city 'consist of bastioned lines in which the bastions, relatively small, are connected by long curtains. The defect of flanking fire in this trace is remedied by the interpolation between the bastions as required, of one or more Martello towers'.[22] Each tower was armed with a single heavy gun, probably a 24pdr, mounted on a traversing platform, and these towers are clearly marked as Martello towers on a Plan of Delhi dated 1857.[23] These towers were about 30ft (9.2m) high with a base diameter of approximately 50ft (15.4m) and were built of small, squared stones. The wall of the tower had a steep batter with a stone string course or cordon marking the level of the gun platform. There was a line of musketry loopholes at ground level and the entrance to the tower was through an opening in the parapet wall. Because these towers were advanced in front of the main city wall they were connected to it by means of a loopholed, three-arched, rubble stone footbridge the end of which was linked to the tower by means of a small drawbridge.

Today only three of the towers remain and, rather strangely, two of these appear to be lower in height than the best preserved one which stands out from the section of wall near the Delhi Gate. However, this disparity in height may well be the result of land in-fill over the last 150 years, since in one of the lower towers a line of loopholes may still be seen at the same level from the top of the tower as the loopholes in the Delhi Gate tower, but today they are so close to the present level of the ground as to be quite unusable for defence.

Built by the British to improve the defences of the old city, these Delhi towers were the only Martello towers which ever saw action. Their effectiveness as defensive structures was amply demonstrated when in 1857 they were held against the British by mutinous sepoys and fire from the towers caused many casualties to the British force. It is ironic then that the only Martello towers to be tested in war had been built by the British only to be defended against the assault of their own designers.

The West Indies and Bermuda

Across the Atlantic a total of four towers were built in the Caribbean and on Bermuda, including one on the small island of Barbuda, today part of the independent state of Antigua and Barbuda in the Lesser Antilles. Predating all the other British towers, the Barbuda tower was built in 1745, to a design closely resembling that of the Spanish towers of the same period, and its construction supports the view that the Spanish towers were then well known to Royal Navy officers.

Situated about 26 miles (40 km) north of Antigua, the importance of Barbuda in the mid-eighteenth century is somewhat difficult to appreciate today. The island has no harbour and in the 1740s a population of only about 500 slaves and overseers on a single plantation owned by the Codrington family. In 1745 the second Sir William Codrington constructed a tower and battery, now known as River Fort, to a plan provided by Commodore Charles Knowles, RN, later Admiral Sir Charles Knowles, who was then commanding the Leeward Islands station. The Codrington papers refer to a proposal to build a tower 'like the Spanish coastal towers', and Knowles's design is almost exactly that.[24] Knowles was an unusual naval officer who, according to a biographical memoir in the Naval Chronicle for 1799: 'Enjoyed the reputation he justly merited, of being an excellent engineer'.[25] In 1741 he was responsible for the fortification of Port Antonio in Jamaica and also for work on the dockyard. It is also believed that he was responsible for the original fortifications of Antigua, an island he knew well, being the first captain to bring a ship-of-the-line into English Harbour.

The Barbuda tower was not only a very early prototype of the later Martello towers and designed by a naval officer, but it was also a tower which was built privately without reference to the Board of Ordnance in London. It was built as a keep for the battery which protected the south-west approach to the main landing place on the island. It was 56ft (17.2m) high, and so was considerably taller than any Martello tower. Built of stone it had a batter to the wall and a base diameter of approximately 46ft (14.15m) narrowing to about 24ft (7.38m) at the parapet. Like the later Martello towers and the Gando tower in the Canary Islands, the tower of River Fort had three levels but, unlike these towers, it had a line of embrasures on each level. There were three separate magazines in the basement and on the first floor there was a fireplace with a flue built into the wall. Entrance to the tower, unlike in any other tower, was below ground level, that is at basement level, and this was probably because Knowles felt that the entrance was adequately protected by the walls of the battery. Access to the upper floors within the tower was by ladder. The armament was probably three 18pdr guns firing through embrasures since, according to the Codrington papers, three such guns were ordered by Sir William Codrington's secretary Colonel King from Lady Codrington in England.[26] Whether these guns were actually mounted in the tower or were part of the battery is uncertain.

River Fort was one of a number of fortifications built on Barbuda by the Codrington family to protect their plantation and to prevent

Plan and section of River Fort, Barbuda. [Greg Cox]

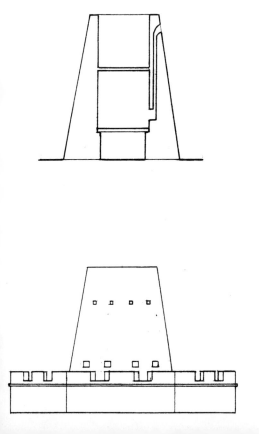

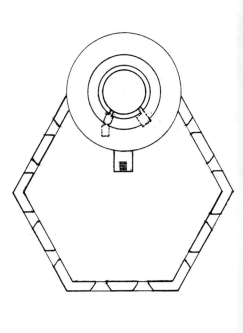

the use of the island by the French for operations against Antigua, then becoming an increasingly important base for the Royal Navy in the eastern Caribbean. The fort stands today as the most impressive structure on Barbuda and is used as a landmark by yachtsmen approaching the island's main landing place.

Two Martello towers were built fifty years later, one on Trinidad and the other on Jamaica. The Trinidad tower was built in 1801 as part of the defences of Abercromby Heights overlooking Port of Spain. Named after Lieutenant-Colonel Thomas Picton, later General Sir Thomas Picton the famous commander of Wellington's Light Division in the Peninsular War, it was also called St. David's Tower and was built of rubble stone faced with stucco. It was 25ft (7.6m) high with a base diameter of 33ft (10.15m), and a diameter at the gun platform of 30ft (9.2m). The tower was circular with a wall 4ft (1.2m) thick, except in one quadrant where the thickness was increased to 6ft (1.8m). According to notes on a plan made by Captain George Lewis, RE shortly after its construction, this portion of the tower 'is thicker than any other part as it might be possible for an Enemy to Establish a battery in [that] direction, but with great difficulty and danger'.[27]

Lewis, who was later in his career to build towers on Jersey and in South Africa, proposed that the tower be armed with one 24pdr carronade to support the battery of four 18pdrs at the foot of the tower, but it is not known whether this armament was ever mounted. There were two lines of loopholes in the wall of the tower, except in

Fort Picton, Port of Spain, Trinidad; completed in 1801, it was one of the earliest towers built by the British. [Author's collection]

the quadrant where its thickness had been increased, and the door was, as usual, at first-floor level. Access to the tower was by means of a ladder and within the tower, as there was no staircase, once again ladders and trapdoors provided access to the gun platform and the ground floor. Half of the ground floor was divided to provide a powder magazine and a storeroom, while in the other half a low, stepped wall was built in a semicircle 2ft (0.6m) out from the wall of the tower to provide an unique cistern within which fresh water was collected from the gun platform.

Fort Picton is probably the earliest one to be built which closely resembled the Martello towers built in England and Ireland four years later. It had, however, a short history and by 1810 it was reported as being abandoned, but a single 12pdr gun was maintained in the nearby battery as an alarm gun.[28] Today the tower is a National Monument, although not well known to the general public. It is now surrounded by one of the poorer suburbs of Port of Spain but is maintained in good order.

The Jamaica tower was constructed between 1808 and 1811 to reinforce the existing defences of Kingston Harbour. Brigadier-General Sir Thomas Shipley, RE had been sent to Jamaica in 1806 to report on the island's defences after a conflict of opinion as to their effectiveness had developed between Sir Eyre Coote, the Governor, and Colonel Ramsey, RE, the Commanding Engineer. Shipley was appalled at the state in which he found the defences, bearing out Ramsey's criticisms, and in his report he stated: 'I can have no hesitation in saying that the Existing Defences are totally inadequate to the Security of the Island'.[29] Shipley had no time whatever for the ideas of the colonial government on defence, as he also stated in his report: 'But it demands imperiously that no more money should be wasted on Irrational Plans, Conceived in Error, Acted upon without Energy, but persisted in, with the Confidence and Obstinacy of Ignorance'.[30] His recommendations for improving the defences of Jamaica were numerous and included a tower to be built on the eastern spur of Long Mountain, overlooking the harbour, to secure that part of the spur which dominated Fort Nugent, as the existing fortification on that site, Fort Castile, had been renamed.

The tower was built by the colonial government of Jamaica and was circular with a distinct batter to the wall. The base diameter was approximately 39ft (11.6m) and the height about 26ft (8m), and so the tower was somewhat smaller than the Kent and the Sussex towers. It was built of cut stone and, again unlike the south-coast towers, had a single machicolation over the doorway and, on the first floor, four

large embrasures. Two of these were
large enough each to take a gun and
the entrance, as with virtually all
Martello towers, was at first-floor
level.[31] Brigadier-General Shipley's
report of 1807 recommended that
one 5½in howitzer should be
mounted on the tower, but a return
of 1811 shows that the armament at
that date was one 12pdr gun on a
traversing platform.[32]

The Jamaica tower had no central
pillar nor bomb-proof arch but,
uniquely, it did have a stone spiral
staircase which, although built partly
into the wall, projected into the interior of the tower. The wall was
insufficiently thick to permit the
staircase to be contained entirely
within it, as in the English and the
Irish towers, so the decision was
taken to enclose the staircase where
it projected into the tower inside a
cut stone wall which stood the full
height of the tower. It may have been
thought that this inner wall would
provide some additional support to
the gun platform.

*The tower at Fort Nugent, Kingston, Jamaica;
the concrete observation post was built on the
gun platform in the late nineteenth century.*
[Author's collection]

The tower was modified at the end of the nineteenth century when
a modern breech-loading 9.2in gun was mounted in Fort Nugent. A
concrete observation post was built on the gun platform of the tower
and a doorway opened at ground level. Today the tower may still be
visited and it stands unused, but in poor condition, overlooking the
Harbour View housing estate in Kingston.

Finally, also across the Atlantic, stood another tower on the strategically situated island of Bermuda off the east coast of the United
States. Bermuda became an important base for the Royal Navy after
the American War of Independence in 1783. A review of the island's
defences in 1823 resulted in the completion in 1828 of a single
Martello tower to protect the Ferry Passage between St. George's
Island and the main island.[33] The Bermuda tower, the construction of
which was supervised by Major Blanshard, RE, was generally similar

to the English south-coast towers although slightly smaller. The tower was built of 'hardstone', a form of local limestone, and was sited within a ditch 18ft (5.5m) wide.

Although resembling the English towers, the design of the Ferry Point tower obviously reflected local circumstances. It was built by convict labour and provided with a staircase within the tower wall from the first to the ground floor. The tower was 34ft (10.5m) high with a maximum diameter of 39ft (12m), and there was no central pillar to support the roof and gun platform. This platform itself was small with a terreplein of 19ft (5.8m) and, unusually, had a narrow walkway between the central masonry mount and the parapet. The iron rail for the traversing platform ran around the perimeter of the central mount rather than along the foot of the parapet as in the English towers. The diameter of the central mount was 12ft 4in (3.8m) and this was large enough to take a standard, central pivot traversing platform, the total length of which was 16ft (4.9m) but with a length between the front and the rear wheels of 10ft (3m). In 1857 the armament of the tower was a single 18pdr gun firing *en barbette*.[34]

The Ferry Point tower was built contemporaneously with Fort St. Catherine, a large battery situated on the northernmost point of St. George's Island. This fort had a D-shaped keep similar to a number of Irish batteries built ten years earlier, including those at Rathmullen on Lough Swilly and Keelogue on the Shannon. The later Fort George, also on St. George's Island and built in the 1840s, had a circular keep mounting 24pdr guns. The Ferry Point tower still exists and, together with Fort St. Catherine, has become a major tourist attraction on the island.

The tower at Ferry Point, St. George's Island, Bermuda. [Bermuda Maritime Museum]

CHAPTER 9

The Final Towers

Wales, England and Guernsey

Although a number of Martello towers were built in the colonies after 1815 none were built in Britain or Ireland between that date and 1840, though five were built on Jersey and completed by 1837. On the continent, however, the use of towers to defend cities and ports continued to find favour, particularly with Austrian engineers. Archduke Maximilian of Austria designed a scheme of defence for the town of Linz in 1832, using forty-two large circular towers, and five more towers were built by the Austrians to defend Verona in northern Italy. In Russia two large circular towers were built to defend Bomarsund on the Aland Islands in the Baltic and the Malakoff Tower was built as part of the fortifications of Sebastopol. So when in the 1840s the British government came under pressure from public opinion to improve the defences of the major naval bases, towers were still in fashion and were once again included in the plans for the new defences.

The pressure of public opinion was due mainly to a combination of increasing French military confidence thirty years after Waterloo and the determination to improve the capability of the French navy by improving its bases, particularly Cherbourg, together with an eager acceptance of the new steam power. On the British side the situation was aggravated by Palmerston's aggressive foreign policy and jingoism so that any attempt by the French to improve their navy was seen by the British government and people as a direct threat to the country's security. In 1846 relations between Britain and France reached a low ebb due to the 'Spanish Marriage', when a close relationship was forged between France and Spain. All this led to a major invasion 'crisis' spurred on by the press and added to in the same year by deteriorating relations with the United States during the dispute over the delineation of the Canadian border.

In 1813 the Admiralty had decided to establish a major dockyard and shipbuilding facility in Wales at Paterchurch, situated at the head of the magnificent natural harbour of Milford Haven in Pembrokeshire. As a result the small town of Pembroke Dock was founded on what today would be called a 'green-field' site. With the shipyard established and rapidly growing in size it became necessary to consider how it should be defended and a study was carried out in 1817 by Major-General Alexander Bryce.[1] In his report he recommended that a number of batteries and three towers should be built, two of them to be sited on the dockyard wall and the third on Stack Rock, a small islet commanding the entrance to Milford Haven. Nothing came of Bryce's report and it was not until twenty-seven years later, in 1844, that a Naval and Military Committee was set up to consider the defences of what had become by then a major naval dockyard.[2]

The committee noted the vulnerable position of Pembroke Dock, situated as it was so far to the west and distant from any main military garrison, for it was only fifty years since the French had landed in this area at Fishguard. Among the committee's recommendations was the revival of the proposal to build two towers to augment the defences of the dockyard, but the committee did not consider Stack Rock suitable for a battery. Construction of the two dockyard towers, the North East Martello Tower and the South West Martello Tower, began in 1848 and in 1850 the committee's views on Stack Rock were disregarded and work started on the building of a three-gun tower on the islet.

All three towers were referred to in Board of Ordnance papers of the time as 'Martello towers' but gone was the Georgian simplicity of

Section of the North East Martello Tower, Pembroke Dock; the tower has been refurbished and is now a museum and tourist information centre. [Author's photograph]

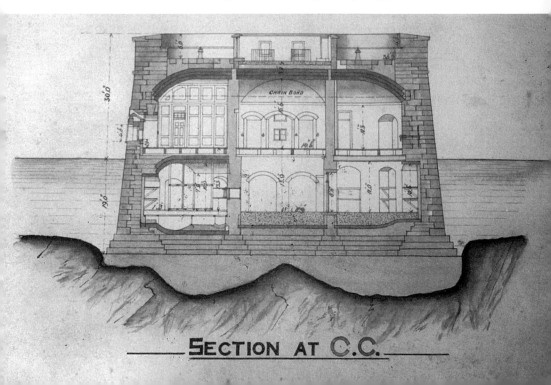

SECTION AT C.C.

The entrance to the North East Martello Tower, showing the later form of machicolation above the doorway. [Author's photograph]

design which marked the towers built at the beginning of the century. The designs of these later towers were each different, one being polygonal, one oval and the third also oval but with a 'return' at the rear

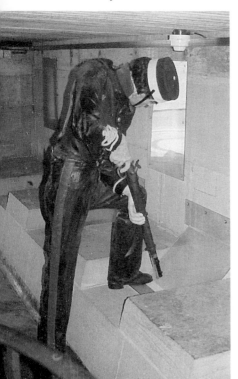

below the level of the gun platform. Built of brick with a limestone facing and granite details, these towers were truly Victorian with embrasures, windows and indented, arched machicolation all of which gave them a somewhat Gothic look. They also reflected the new building technology of the time and the gun platforms were supported by iron girders rather than a central brick pillar. The total cost of the two dockyard towers came to £9,230.

Construction of the Pembroke Dock towers was prolonged, taking from 1848 to 1851, and there was considerable correspondence between the Inspector General of Fortifications and the

Here we see how the defenders of the North East Martello Tower would have been able to fire down through the loopholes in the floor of the machicolation on an enemy attacking the tower entrance. [Author's photograph]

commanding engineer at Pembroke Dock complaining at the slowness of the contractor.[3] The Pembroke Dock towers were sited on the beach adjoining the dockyard wall and at high tide both were surrounded by water. Although the South West Tower was taller, being 52ft (16m) compared with 49ft (15m) for the North East Tower, the latter was the larger overall and mounted three 32pdr guns on the gun platform while the South West Tower mounted only one. Both towers were sited to provide enfilade fire along the dockyard wall and, in addition to the 32pdr guns, each had a secondary armament of 12pdr brass howitzers inside the tower and firing through embrasures, three in the North East Tower and four in the South West Tower.

Because the gun platforms of the towers had been designed by the engineers without reference to the Director General of Artillery, it was found on their completion that they would not take the standard pattern traversing platforms for the guns since the radii of the racers did not correspond with the established pattern of traversing platforms. As a result, after another round of rather acrimonious correspondence, this time between the Inspector General of Fortifications and the Director General of Artillery, four special iron traversing platforms had to be manufactured by the Royal Carriage Department and the armament was not finally mounted until 1855.[4] The North East Tower was provided with a shot furnace but neither the guns nor the furnace was ever used in war. It was not until the Second World War when two .303in Lewis anti-aircraft machine-guns

The gun platform of the North East Martello Tower; the picture shows positions for the three 32pdr guns; the weapon in the picture is an 18pdr Blomefield gun mounted on a reproduction carriage and traversing platform. [Author's photograph]

were mounted on the gun platform of the North East Tower that either of these towers engaged an enemy, in this case German aircraft attacking Pembroke Dock. Today the North East Tower has been refurbished and is in use as a tourist information centre while the South West Tower is closed up but remains in relatively good condition.

The third tower at Milford Haven, the Stack Rock Tower, was designed to mount three 32pdr guns. Situated on a small islet 500yd (460m) off South Hook Point, its position enabled it to control access for ships to Man of War Roads and Pembroke Dock. The tower was oval in shape with a diameter of 55ft (16.9m) at its longest axis, but its height differed between front and rear because of a variation in the level of the rock on which it was built. At the front the tower had a height of 21ft (6.46m) but at the rear this increased to 30ft (9.2m).

Tenders for the construction of the tower were called for in 1850 and the tower was completed by 1854 at a cost of £8,740.[5] However,

Stack Rock Fort as it is today, showing the original three-gun tower encircled by the casemates constructed in 1870. [Crown Copyright: Royal Commission on the Ancient and Historic Monuments of Wales]

The Brehon Tower off Guernsey. Completed in 1856 the tower guarded the shipping channel between Guernsey and the smaller island of Herm. [P.G. Laker Esq.]

the life of the tower was short because of the anti-French fever sweeping the country, which in 1858 resulted in the setting up of a special committee by the Secretary of State for War to consider the defences of Milford Haven. The committee included the noted naval gunnery expert Captain Cooper Key, RN and the equally well known expert on fortifications Major Jervois, RE. One of the committee's recommendations was the replacement of the tower on Stack Rock by a larger fort. Although work had actually started on a two-tiered fort by 1859, this proposal was subsequently subsumed in the recommendations of the 1859 Royal Commission which reported on the defences of the United Kingdom as a whole. Work on the fort was delayed by changes in the design resulting from technical advances in armour and artillery occurring at that time, but eventually, between 1865 and 1871, the larger fort was completed by constructing a single tier of sixteen casemates around the original tower. It was adapted for use as part of the garrison's living accommodation in the new fort and became the officers' mess. It may still be seen today by anyone visiting the fort.

The last two towers to be built in the United Kingdom, a three-gun tower on the Spit of Grain opposite Sheerness in Kent and the Brehon Tower off Guernsey, were built between 1854 and 1857. The Grain Tower was built as part of the continuing effort to improve the defences of the Medway while the Brehon Tower was a result of the fortification of the Channel Islands to counter the recently fortified

The Spit of Grain Tower, opposite Sheerness, showing the alterations and additions made to it in two world wars; the chain around the base is a remnant of the Medway boom defence.
[Author's photograph]

French port and naval base of Cherbourg. Construction of a tower on the Spit of Grain had been suggested six years earlier in 1848, but it was not until 1854 that work was carried out to maintain and secure the foundations which had previously been laid and then neglected. The tower itself was not completed until 1856-57 at a cost of £16,798, a very large sum for a tower this size and which probably reflected the difficulties experienced in providing adequate foundations.[6]

The Spit of Grain Tower was also oval in plan with a base of 71ft (21.8m) by 63ft (19.3m), with a height of 42ft (12.9m) and a wall 12ft (3.69m) thick. The armament was one 56pdr gun and two 32pdr guns; these guns remained the armament of the tower as late as 1910 when it was disarmed and then used as a communications tower. In 1915, during the First World War, the gun platform was altered to mount two 4.7in QF guns while the base of the tower was used to secure one end of the Medway boom defence. The 4.7in guns were removed soon after the war ended but at the beginning of the Second World War the tower was brought into use once again. This time it was rearmed with two 6pdr QF guns and additional barrack accommodation was built on concrete pillars alongside the tower together with a tall fire control post on the gun platform. This is how the tower remains today, unused and derelict.[7]

Like the Stack Rock Tower, the Spit of Grain Tower was considered by the 1859 Commission to be too small and weak to be fully effective and it was recommended that the tower should be enclosed by a casemated fort. However, the recommendations of the Commission when fully costed came to the staggering sum of £11 million and even

Palmerston's enthusiasm for fortifications was somewhat diminished when ways of raising this enormous sum were considered, particularly as his Chancellor of the Exchequer (W.E. Gladstone) was strongly opposed to the whole scheme. A review of the Commission's recommendations was carried out which resulted in a saving of £3 million, and among the works cancelled was the proposal to enclose the Spit of Grain Tower within a larger fort.[8]

The Brehon Tower was built on a rock in the channel through the Little Russel, halfway between Guernsey and the island of Herm. The building of the tower started in 1854 with the intention that it should control the main shipping channel between the two islands and it was completed in 1856 at a cost of £8,098.18s.10d.[9] It was a large oval tower, measuring 65ft (20m) by 85ft (26.16m) at its broadest point and was built of granite ashlar on three levels. The ground floor contained the magazine, shifting room, shell room, artillery and provision stores and a large fresh water cistern. The cistern was fed with rain water through pipes running down from the gun platform. Latrines were also situated on the ground floor and their provision reflected not only the isolation of the tower but also the advances in Victorian plumbing. Access to all floors was by means of a stone spiral staircase and the first floor contained a number of rooms providing the living quarters for the garrison.

The tower had a single doorway at first-floor level and at intervals around the parapet there were six small, machicolated galleries, but none directly over the doorway. The armament was originally designed to be mounted on two levels with three heavy guns on the gun platform and a lower battery of five guns and nine spare embrasures. With this large armament it was planned that the garrison should be two officers and sixty NCOs and soldiers. Before the tower was completed, however, the armament was modified to five guns on the gun platform, three 68pdr guns and two 10in shell guns and the garrison was reduced to two officers and thirty men.[10] These guns were removed by the end of the century when the tower was evacuated, but it found a new lease of life between 1940 and 1945 when the German Army occupied the Channel Islands and an anti-aircraft battery was positioned on the tower. Today it stands in reasonable condition, a landmark to the many tourists arriving in St. Peter Port by sea and visited only by local yachtsmen and fishermen.

These five towers - at Milford Haven, on the Spit of Grain and off Guernsey - though not themselves true examples of the original Martello design, were, in fact, the logical extension of this design to meet the changing circumstances of the mid-nineteenth century.

The Overseas Towers

Some of the last Martello towers were built overseas between 1839 and 1855. Nine towers altogether were constructed: one on the island of Corfu in the Adriatic, six in Canada and one each in South Africa and Australia. The tower on Corfu was the first of these towers to be built and was completed in 1839 as part of the defences protecting the important British base on the island. This was followed by the Canadian towers which were built to defend the city of Kingston on the shores of Lake Ontario. The South African tower was part of the frontier defences of Eastern Cape Province, and the Australian tower defended Sydney harbour.

Corfu, because of its strategic position guarding the entrance to the Adriatic Sea, had long been fortified. Held by the Venetians from 1203 to 1797, it was lost to the French in that year and then occupied by a Turco-Russian force from 1799 to 1807. The modern fortifications on the island, however, date from the second French occupation in 1807 when the island was ceded to France under the Treaty of Tilsit before passing to Great Britain in 1815 under the Treaty of Paris.

The French occupation had resulted in the construction of a number of modern fortifications in the town of Corfu itself and on the small island of Vido lying some 1,000yd (960m) offshore from the town. The Venetian, the Russian and the French navy all saw the vital importance of holding Vido if Corfu was to be successfully defended against an enemy attack, and in this view the British concurred.

In 1822 a young Royal Engineers officer stationed on Corfu, Lieutenant Worsley, suggested a radical solution to the problem of improving the fortifications of Vido in a report on the defences ordered by the Duke of Wellington. He recommended that all the French and the older Venetian fortifications should be pulled down or blown up and that two large new works and a tower should be built in their place. This plan was accepted by the Board of Ordnance and resulted in the demolition of the French-built Signal and Napoleon redoubts and in their places the erection of Fort George, a large pentagonal fort, and the Wellington Lunette. In the north of the island there was a small cove and landing place defended by an old Venetian hexagonal work built about 1730 and called Fort Schulemburg. It was here that Worsley proposed the construction of a four-gun tower to be named Maitland Tower. The original design was for one similar to Tower CC at Aldeburgh and sited within a ditch, but with a casemated gallery leading to the small cove.[11]

Unusually for the nineteenth century, the fortifications on Vido were to be constructed under conditions of considerable secrecy and the building of Fort George and the Wellington Lunette were begun soon after the submission of Worsley's report to London. This speed in authorizing and starting the work was, perhaps, an indication of the importance placed on the defence of Corfu by the British government. Certainly work on the defences had begun by 1824, the year when Colonel Sir John Jones, RE and Lieutenant-Colonel Whitmore, RE were ordered to the island to provide a further report on the defences. Although their report resulted in a radical review of how Corfu should be defended in future it did not affect the works being built on Vido, although it may have contributed to the delay in the starting of work on the Maitland Tower.

That did not begin until 1833 and then it was to a different design from that originally proposed in 1822 by Lieutenant Worsley. The new design was for a large, circular tower in place of the earlier four-lobed design, but still mounting the same armament of four guns. It was to have a diameter of about 65ft (20m) and to contain a magazine for 156 barrels of gunpowder and a water tank with a capacity of 17,798 gallons. The armament proposed for the tower in 1839 was two 8in shell guns and two 24pdr 'heavy' guns.[12]

The cost of the tower was estimated at £5,000 and the total cost of the new works on Vido came to a total of £53,000, a large sum of money which could now be described quite accurately as totally wasted because twenty years later the British government took the decision to hand Corfu and the other Ionian Islands to the Kingdom of Greece. Before the handing over it was planned to destroy all the fortifications to prevent any future use of the island as a military base. However, there was considerable opposition to this plan from the local inhabitants: since the Corfiotes felt that the building of the fortifications had been financed largely by local taxes they believed that they had a pecuniary interest in their fate. The Lord High Commissioner, Viscount Kirkwall, had considerable sympathy with their view and together their opposition persuaded the War Department that only a part of the fortifications of the town and all those so recently constructed on Vido should be demolished.

In his plan for the destruction of the Maitland Tower Major de Vere, RE proposed that the demolition should 'be effected by driving galleries from the large tank in its centre, under the four great piers supporting the arches of the building, and there lodging heavy charges the explosion of which would render the tower a heap of ruins'.[13] In March 1864 this was done and the Maitland Tower was blown up.

In Canada the importance of Kingston for control of the country was brought home to the British after the unsuccessful attack on the town by the Americans in 1812. It was recognized in 1840 that command of Lake Ontario depended on holding Kingston and its vital dockyard and their loss would have meant loss of control of the lakes and probably too the ultimate loss of Quebec and all Canada. Despite the city's obvious importance and its proximity to the American naval base across Lake Ontario at Sackets Harbor, no attempt was made by the British authorities to improve Kingston's temporary fortifications after the war ended in 1815. In 1825 the Duke of Wellington set up a commission under the direction of Major-General Sir James Carmichael-Smyth, RE, who as Commanding Engineer North Britain in 1809 had been involved in the early stages of the construction of the Leith tower. He was instructed to review all the defence requirements of 'His Majesty's North American Provinces'. The report of the Smyth Commission reviewed the possible enemy approaches to Canada, which in practice meant the three main lines of communication from the United States. These were along the Richlieu River to Montreal and Quebec, across Lake Ontario to Kingston and then to Ottawa or via Niagara to Toronto.

The Commission recommended the construction of a number of strategically sited, permanent forts and, in addition, the building of the Rideau Canal system.[14] This canal was designed to provide secure passage for British vessels between Montreal and Kingston, enabling them to avoid the international boundary with the United States which, between those points, was drawn along the middle of the narrowest section of the St. Lawrence River. Although the Treasury approved its construction it refused to sanction the elaborate scheme of defences originally proposed to defend the canal, the city of Kingston and the dockyard. It was not until 1832 when the canal was completed that a modified scheme was approved which included Fort Henry, a number of redoubts and the six towers. Construction of these

The Martello tower at Fort Frederick, Kingston, Ontario; the tower was surrounded by a ditch which was defended by bulbous caponiers projecting into it from the base of the tower. [Author's collection]

new defences was spurred on in 1844 with the election of Senator James K. Polk as President of the United States. Polk had campaigned on a jingoistic ticket with a demand that the whole Oregon Territory should be included in the United States. The 'Oregon crisis' in 1845 brought the imminent threat of another war with the USA and forced the British government to review the woefully weak defences of its North American colonies; the result was the reactivation of the earlier proposal to build a number of Martello towers as a cheap and speedy demonstration of the government's intention to defend them.

The four large towers built at Kingston (the Fort Frederick Tower, the Murney Tower, the Cedar Island Tower and the Shoal Tower) were the largest built to the original Martello design and in 1850 their design incorporated the latest ideas in fortification to enable a masonry tower to withstand attack. The towers were sited in an arc across the entrance to the Rideau Canal with the Murney Tower, the most westerly, protecting Kingston itself, and the Shoal Tower 300yd (260m) further north and actually standing in the waters of the harbour. However, the Point Frederick position was the key to the defence of Kingston, located as it was between the canal entrance and the dockyard. Here a tower was built to act as a keep and barrack for Fort Frederick while the fourth tower, on Cedar Island, defended the eastern approach to the dockyard.

Designed to act as both a keep and a barrack, the tower on Point Frederick had three storeys rather than two as in the other towers and, like the Murney and the Cedar Island Tower, was surrounded by a ditch scarped with masonry. The bases of all three towers were defended by four bulbous caponiers projecting into the ditch, and these removed the need to provide machicolation at parapet level to cover the bases of the towers. The gun platform of the Murney Tower was circular and the tower was designed to mount two guns, using a single pivot, while the other towers had trefoil-shaped gun platforms, as in the English east-coast towers, and were designed to mount three guns each. Because of the severe climate each of the towers was later covered by a conical timber roof to protect the gun platform from snow. This roof was designed in sections so that it could be removed when the guns were to be fired.

The dimensions of these large towers were not uniform and varied from the smaller Cedar Island and the Murney Tower, each with a base diameter of approximately 54ft (16.6m) and a height of 36ft (11m), to the larger Fort Frederick Tower with a base diameter of 60ft (18.4m) and a height of 45ft (13.8m). The Shoal Tower, constructed in shallow water about 100yd (92m) from the Kingston waterfront, had a base diameter of 65ft (20m) and a height of 35ft (10.7m). The increase in the size of the Kingston towers when compared with the earlier English ones was necessary because of the increased number and size of the guns mounted on them and the additional storage room required. Instead of simply a magazine and a store, as in the early towers, the basement of each of the Kingston towers now provided space not only for a magazine but also for a commissariat store, two ordnance stores, a barrack store and a fresh-water cistern. However, because of its situation, the Shoal Tower was not provided with a cistern.

The arming of the towers became a long drawn-out saga which was not finally resolved until 1863, fifteen years after their completion. The Murney Tower was originally intended to mount two 24pdr guns, a standard gun 9ft 6in (2.9m) in overall length and a short gun of 6ft (1.8m), each on a dwarf traversing carriage. The other towers were to mount three guns each, two standard 32pdr guns and one short 24 pdr; this accounted for the trefoil-shaped gun platform with three separate pivots. However, as with the Pembroke Dock towers in Wales, there was a lack of liaison between the Engineer Department and the Artillery Department in Canada and the latter insisted that the towers should be armed solely with the more powerful 32pdr guns. The dimensions of the gun platforms did not permit the use of standard traversing platforms for all three guns and the matter became the subject of acrimonious correspondence between the branches of the Ordnance Department and the Royal Carriage Department in London.

Eventually the decision was taken to alter the gun platforms of each tower to enable the standard traversing platforms to be used, but this argument delayed the actual decision until 1852, and there were further delays until 1863 before the the platforms were finally manu-factured, delivered to Canada and the guns mounted. The final armament of the Fort Frederick Tower was three 32pdr guns on the gun platform and six 32pdr carronades mounted within the tower. The Cedar Island and the Shoal Tower had a similar armament on the gun platform but mounted only three carronades inside the tower, while the Murney Tower was armed with two 32pdr guns and two 32pdr carronades.

These four towers were particularly impressive to look at and most probably reflected the most advanced level of gun-tower design constructed anywhere in the British Empire. Today all the towers remain and two are museums and open to the public. The Fort Frederick Tower has been the museum of the Royal Military College of Canada since the 1920s and the Murney Tower is the museum of the Kingston Historical Society.

Two smaller towers were also built as part of the defences of Fort Henry, a fort on the promontory west of Fort Frederick which had been completed in 1836 as a result of the report of the Smyth Commission in 1825. The towers at Fort Henry were not true Martello towers, having neither a magazine nor accommodation for a permanent garrison. Rather they were designed to provide protection for the ditches flanking the fort and flanking fire along the shoreline of the lake which could not be covered by fire from the fort itself. The towers, known as the East and the West Branch Ditch Tower were 45ft (13.8m) high and 30ft (9.25m) in diameter, with walls 8ft (2.5m) thick on the side facing the lake, but on the landward side the thickness was reduced to 2ft (0.6m). Part of the reason for this reduction was to enable the guns of the fort to destroy the towers should they be captured by the enemy. The walls had embrasures and loopholes

Plan and section of a Branch Ditch tower at Fort Henry, Kingston, Ontario. [National Archives of Canada, NMC13535]

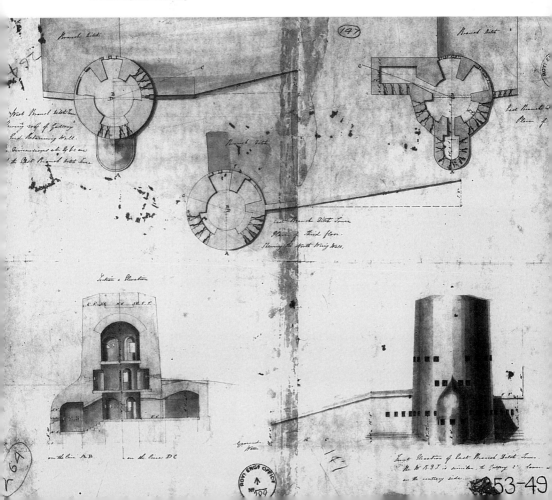

and there was a small, loopholed caponier covering the shoreline. On the gun platform there was one 24pdr gun mounted on a dwarf traversing platform and the gun had a 360-degree traverse. These interesting towers may still be seen as part of Fort Henry, itself now a major Canadian heritage site.[15]

Many thousands of miles away in the southern hemisphere a number of towers were built in Eastern Cape Province in the colony of the Cape of Good Hope, now South Africa. In the 1830s the British colonial government tried to restrict Boer expansion into Xhosa or, as they were called by the British, Kaffir lands in the east of the colony. British troops were used to police the eastern frontier but were unable to prevent Boer hunger for land leading to the Sixth Frontier War of 1833-34. The constant raiding across the frontier and the generally unsettled state of the country led to a plan to establish a line of forts or defensible barracks along the eastern frontier.

The commanding engineer, Lieutenant-Colonel Lewis, RE, produced a report in 1837 which recommended the construction of a line of redoubts, defensible barracks, single-gun towers and what were termed 'Picket Towers' to protect the frontier.[16] Five single-gun towers were recommended, three for the defence of Grahamstown and two at Fort Beaufort, with picket towers at Fort Brown, Fort Peddie, Trumpeter's Drift, Committee Drift and a number of other locations. The Inspector General of Fortifications, at that time Major-General Mulcaster, believed, however, that only defensible barracks and picket towers were necessary. In a letter to the Secretary of State, dated 27 February 1839, Mulcaster, who himself had served in Minorca in 1798-99 as lieutenant and captain, wrote: 'I recommend Colonel Lewis's system of Defensible Barracks with the small Picquet Towers for approval, these small towers are essentially parts of the

The tower at Fort Beaufort, Eastern Cape Province, South Africa. [Author's collection]

defensible loopholed Barrack system.'[17]

The Picket towers were small rectangular structures, about 25ft (7.6m) high and designed, according to Colonel Lewis, writing later in the *Professional Papers of the Royal Engineers*, to act as keeps or flank defences to the defensible barracks. The towers had a single line of musketry loopholes on the first floor and the majority of the towers were defended with a field piece. A few, however, mounted a single 5$\frac{1}{2}$in iron howitzer on the roof platform. The cost of a picket tower was estimated at £873.12s.3$\frac{1}{2}$d.[18]

Although General Mulcaster did not recommend the construction of the larger single-gun towers, by 1839 the building of one of the two proposed for Fort Beaufort had already commenced. The tower was eventually completed in 1846 and stood 31ft (9.5m) high and had a base diameter of 32ft (9.8m). It had a batter to the wall and a single machicolation over the door which was at first-floor level. It was a round tower built of ashlar masonry and had a central masonry pillar supporting the bomb-proof gun platform. The first floor had four windows which also acted as embrasures and access to each floor was by means of a wooden spiral staircase built partly into the wall. The ground floor, or basement, was divided into two parts by a thick brick wall built on either side of the central pillar which formed two separate rooms, one a storeroom and the other the magazine. The tower mounted one gun, a 5$\frac{1}{2}$in iron howitzer on a traversing platform; the cost of building the tower was £1,169.11s.4d. The tower was garrisoned during the Seventh Frontier War, or 'The War of the Axe', which lasted from 1846 to 1847 during which, on one occasion, Fort Beaufort was briefly besieged. However, the lightly-armed Xhosa, unable to deal with fortifications without artillery, eventually withdrew. The tower is still standing and is maintained by the South African National Monuments Council.

The last tower of all, however, was constructed as part of Fort Denison in Sydney harbour in Australia. As with many other Martello towers, the Fort Denison tower was part of a fort which was built in 1855 to defend the inner harbour at Sydney. It was built on Pinchgut Island, a small island in the middle of the harbour, and it is said that the decision to use Pinchgut Island resulted from an unannounced visit to Sydney by two American naval vessels in December 1839. The ships concerned were the sloops-of-war the USS *Vincennes* and the USS *Peacock* which were part of the United States' Exploring Expedition commanded by Lieutenant Charles Wilkes, USN. These vessels sailed into Sydney harbour on 1 December without being challenged, an event which brought home to the colonial government the vulnerability of one of Australia's two most important cities. In 1841 Pinchgut Island was levelled in preparation for the building of a battery, but after the removal of its top work languished until the outbreak of the Crimean War in 1854, and it was fear of the Russian Pacific Fleet which led to the completion of the battery and tower in 1857.

The sandstone tower was approximately 46ft (14.15m) high with a diameter of 50ft (15.38m). The wall of the tower was 13ft (4m) thick at the base narrowing to 9ft 9in (3m) at the top, and a single 8in shell gun was mounted on the gun platform. The tower had two storeys; the ground floor housed the magazine and the first floor was a gun room for three 32pdr guns firing through embrasures. These guns were installed during the construction of the tower and, once installed, could not easily be removed. The floor of the gun room was supported underneath by a central pillar which was necessary to enable the floor to take the weight of the three guns. The tower acted as a keep for the battery of nine 32pdr guns and two 10in shell guns, but there was separate barrack accommodation in the fort for the gunners. The battery and tower cost £17,000 to construct.[19]

By 1865 the advent of rifled guns with longer ranges resulted in a change in tactics from defence of the inner to defence of the outer harbour at Sydney and Fort Denison became obselete, but it continued to be manned until the 1880s. Today the tower and fort are managed by the New South Wales' Parks and Wildlife Service as a tourist attraction.

Fort Denison in Sydney Harbour, Australia; this was the last Martello tower to be built in the British Empire. [Author's collection]

CHAPTER 10

The Towers that Never Were

Although the towers described in the previous chapter were the last gun towers to be built, their popularity as a means of coastal defence was such that in the period from 1800 to 1860 numerous towers were planned but not subsequently built. Indeed, between 1803 and 1808 there were a number of proposals to extend the line of towers on the east coast of England. Three towers were proposed for the defence of Lowestoft but these were not built, and five years later there was a further suggestion that two Martello towers and a four-gun battery should be built, but once again no action was taken. At the same time four towers were proposed for the protection of Great Yarmouth and again nothing came of this proposal, probably because the threat of invasion in that area had diminished with the defeat of the French at Trafalgar in 1805.[1]

In Ireland between 1800 and 1815 a number of towers were proposed, beginning in 1803 with the Twiss Report's proposal for two square towers for the defence of Enniskillen. There is also reference in a return of 1804, which listed the towers and batteries which the Lord Lieutenant had ordered to be constructed, to two towers to protect Belfast Lough and one each at Oysterhaven, between Cork Harbour and Kinsale, and at Youghal.[2] There is no indication that these were ever built, nor, indeed, was a third tower proposed in 1810 for Duncannon Fort. This tower was: 'To cover the entrance and intended to be the same as those ordered for the heights above the fort'.[3]

In 1811 two quadrangular, or cam-shaped, towers were proposed for Mournes Hill at Athlone and Keelogue on the Shannon.[4] In addition to the quadrangular tower at Athlone, Major-General Fyers, RE suggested in 1814 that 'A Tower of the largest order for four 24pdr guns similar to that constructed at Aldeburgh' should be built at Anchor's Bower, also at Athlone. Although at first receiving the approval of the Board of Ordnance, this tower was not proceeded with as the Board had doubts as to whether there was sufficient space on the site for such a large structure. A tower was also proposed for Packenham Redoubt at Tarbert at the mouth of the Shannon. Once again, none of these towers were built, but at Keelogue and Tarbert the plan was changed to a battery with a defensible guard house. The Keelogue defences were completed in 1817 with a much larger armament of seven guns in the battery and two on the roof of the guardhouse.

Additional towers were also planned for Scotland when in 1807 a letter from the Board reported that the estimates for the year included the sums of £3,344.16s.6d for a tower on Cramond Island and £5,544.16s.6d for another on Inchkeith, both in the Firth of Forth.[5] Unlike the tower on the Beacon Rock at Leith, these two towers were to be built by the Royal Engineers, but Lord Moira, considering the plan, decided that 'The works at Cramond and Inch Keith are not a pressing Description, but may be deferred without material Inconvenience to the Service' and so neither was built.[6] Nor was the second tower planned for Leith Harbour, which was to have been built at the end of a new pier which the Edinburgh Corporation intended to build at Newhaven but which was not actually built until more than a century later, in the 1930s.[7]

In 1806 in the Channel Islands one of the first acts of Lieutenant-General Sir George Don, the newly arrived Lieutenant Governor of Jersey, was to carry out a study of the defences of the island. His report stated: 'Round towers (such as those lately built on the coasts of Sussex and Kent) I am of opinion should be built without delay.' These towers were to be built in the main bays of the island but, as we have seen, only three smaller ones were eventually built.[8] In addition to the towers for the bays around the island, two others were proposed as part of the defences of Fort Regent, the main fortress on the island, built in 1806 on Tower Hill overlooking the harbour of St. Helier. They were planned to secure a hill close to Fort Regent but the plan was cancelled before work had started on them.

Four towers were planned, however, in the 1840s for Guernsey to protect the proposed 'Harbour of Refuge' in Fermain Bay. These were to have been large towers, mounting four heavy guns and with a garrison of sixty men each and were to have been sited in a line across the Jerbourg Peninsula; but the cancellation of the proposed harbour meant that there was no longer any need for these towers. Another one in Guernsey was proposed to reinforce Fort Pembroke in Ancresse Bay, but this was another proposal that was never implemented.[9]

Finally, in 1847, the fortification by the French of the Iles Chausey covering the entrance to St. Malo sent a frisson of fear through the military establishment on Jersey. Immediately a proposal for the fortifying of the uninhabited Ecrehou Islands to the east of Jersey was sent to the Board of Ordnance and the Admiralty. The proposal was for two large Martello towers mounting 32pdr guns to be constructed on Maitre Ile and Marmoutier. The Admiralty did not consider the towers to be necessary and even Palmerston, normally an aggressive proponent of all moves to assert sovereignty - which fortification of the Ecrehous would have been - baulked at spending £10,000 or more on the two towers and they too were never built.[10]

No Martello towers were ever built on Alderney, although two 'Sussex towers' were proposed in 1810 by Major-General John Doyle, the Lieutenant Governor of Guernsey, one to be built on Houmet de Longis (Raz Island), protecting the entrance to Longy Bay, and one at Mannez, to defend the beach nearby.[11] However, in spite of the outbreak of war with the United States in 1812, no action was taken to authorize these towers and with the fall of Napoleon in 1815 there no longer appeared to be any pressing reason to fortify the island. As we have seen, this situation changed in the 1840s and there were again proposals to build Martello towers on Hommett, Longy, Rat (Raz) Island and also at Chateau L'Etoc. Plans for these towers were eventally superseded by more elaborate masonry forts without towers as part of the increased fortification of the island at that time, and in conjunction with the 'Harbours of Refuge' then being built.

Like Alderney, the Isles of Scilly were never defended by Martello towers, although in 1803 Major Lyman, the commanding officer of the troops on the Scillies, wrote to Headquarters, Western District asking for permission to build 'three round towers of about 20ft [6.15m] high and 18 or 20ft [5.5 or 6.15m] in diameter'.[12] Each tower was to have one 32pdr carronade mounted on top and 'with eight or ten men would effectively secure the Garrison from the enemy making any sudden approaches'.[13] Although Lieutenant-General Simcoe, commanding Western District, approved the proposal with reservations, the towers, probably in design more like the early Guernsey examples than Martello towers, became the subject of dispute between Lyman and Captain Marsh, RN, the senior naval officer. Marsh believed the island's garrison was inadequate to man the towers and thought that the principal means of defence should be gunboats manned by Sea Fencibles. It appears that the naval argument carried the day and the towers were never built. The towers on St. Mary's which may be seen today are, in fact, an Admiralty signal tower at Newford Down, built in 1812, and three windmills, one on the Garrison, one at Buzza, and one at Peninnis.[14]

In 1825 a report on the defences of Sheerness proposed a two-gun tower for Barrow's Hill which overlooked the Queenborough Lines and Queenborough itself. This tower was to have been 32ft (9.84m)

Section of the tower poposed for the defence of Barrow's Hill, Sheerness in 1825. [PRO MR 1339(1)]

high with a base diameter of 50ft (15.38m) and a surrounding ditch. An interesting feature would have been the four machicolated galleries built not, as was more usual, at parapet level but in this case 13ft (4m) above the level of the floor of the ditch. The tower was to have been entered across an iron bridge with a retractable end-section and so through one of the machicolated galleries.[15]

Fourteen years later, in 1839, the defences of the east coast were once again reviewed and a large Martello tower was considered for the defence of the small port of Blakeney in Norfolk. This would have cost £7,000, and a second tower, to be armed with three 24pdr guns and a single 32pdr carronade, was suggested to replace the by now derelict Yarmouth Fort.[16]

In 1844 the Naval and Military Committee which reported on the defences of Milford Haven and Pembroke Dock proposed a further three towers in addition to the two dockyard towers and the tower on Stack Rock. A two-gun tower was proposed for Llanreath Point, about 500yd (460m) south-west of the dockyard, and two other towers to prevent access to the Daugleddau River, one on Hobb's Point north of the dockyard and one on Neyland Point on the opposite bank.[17] Construction of these towers was not proceeded with but proposals for building defence towers continued to be made as late as 1859 when the Royal Commission proposed two three-gun towers for the defence of the Isle of Wight at Brook and Brightstone and four towers to improve the defences of Cork Harbour, three on the shores of Ballycotton Bay and one at Ringabella Cove.[18] By 1860, however, the vulnerability of masonry towers to rifled guns was becoming apparent, and when the enormous cost of fully implementing the report of the Royal Commission was considered, particularly in the light of improved relations with France, their construction was cancelled as an economy measure.

Overseas, Martello towers had been planned as early as 1801 for the defence of Port of Spain in Trinidad by Lieutenant-Colonel Shipley, RE, then Commanding Engineer at Martinique.[19] The same officer, now promoted to brigadier-general, suggested a second tower in Jamaica to cover the approaches to the dockyard and to be linked by means of covered communications to Prince William Henry's Polygon.[20] In 1809 towers had been suggested as part of the defences of the dockyard at Bermuda, including one to be sited in the centre of the defensive ditch at the southern end of the dockyard.[21] None of these towers were subsequently built, but in 1822 two towers were proposed for the defence of Ferry Passage between St. George's Island and the main island, but one was cancelled in 1824 by the Commanding Engineer, Major Thomas Blanshard, RE. In a letter Blanshard wrote: 'The Ferry...is to be defended by two Martello towers but I agree with Major Cunningham that only one should be built.'[22] Two other towers had been planned for the dockyard defences, including one on the flank of the defensive ditch across Ireland Island protecting the dockyard from an attack from the west, and a second, larger one at the extreme point. Neither of these towers was built, the recommendation being that, for the tower on the flank

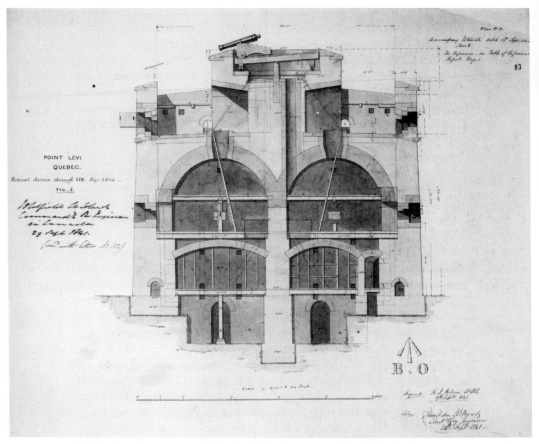

Design for a large tower at Point Levi, Quebec; prepared in 1841, the six towers appear to be modelled on the Napoleonic Tours Modeles *rather than the British Martello towers since they are square in shape and resemble small forts.* [PRO MPH 902]

of the ditch, 'a barrack or caponiere should be substituted for it'.[23]

In Ceylon (Sri Lanka) in 1817 three towers were under construction or proposed for the defence of the port of Trincomalee. Six years earlier, in 1811, a committee comprising Generals Brownrigg and Maitland and Vice-Admiral Hood summoned Lieutenant-Colonel Bridges, previously the Commanding Engineer in Ceylon, to advise it on what defences should be built to protect Trincomalee harbour which, at that time, was defended only by the old Dutch Fort Ostenburgh. Bridges recommended two towers to defend the high ground overlooking Fort Ostenburgh and one tower for a single 24pdr gun, referred to in 1817 by Lieutenant-Colonel Henry Watts, RE as a

'Mortella Tower', to be erected on Clappenburgh Island.[24]

The two towers on the mainland were named after members of the original committee which authorized the new defences: 'Admiral Hood's Tower' was sited on the southern side of Nicholson's Cove across the bay from Fort Ostenburgh, and unusually, this was to have been a square tower; 'General Brownrigg's Tower', north of Nicholson's Cove and to the rear of the fort, was designed as a circular, bomb-proof tower. In 1817 work had started on the two towers and when stopped, in April of that year, the wall of 'Admiral Hood's Tower' had reached a height of 10ft (3m) and the storeroom and tank were complete; but the wall of 'General Brownrigg's Tower' was only 4ft (1.2m) high. Despite urgent pleading by the commanding engineer, Lieutenant-Colonel Watts, that all the materials needed to complete the towers had been assembled they were never finished.[25]

Twelve years later another sapper officer, Captain Henry Brandreth, suggested the building of three handsome, two-gun Martello towers on Ascension Island in the south Atlantic, when he was sent there in 1829 on secondment to the Admiralty. Brandreth was to report on what barrack accommodation and defences should be provided for the garrison and he returned to Ascension the following year to supervise the building works, including the island's water supply and two small batteries. His orders were to supervise the construction of the batteries with the proviso that 'Other works and towers may be proceeded on when these [the batteries] are finished'. In sketches of the island entitled 'Picturesque Views in the Island of Ascension' made in 1835 by Lieutenant William Allen, RN, FRGS the new barracks, hospital and Fort Thornton are all depicted but there is no indication of any towers nor are any shown in the map of the island made by Lieutenant G.A. Bedford, RN in 1838, so that it would seem that they were never built.[26]

After the completion of the tower at Freetown in Sierra Leone in 1805, the Sierra Leone Company proposed building a further two towers, one as a keep for the existing battery and the other across the bay. The cost of the two was estimated at between £5,000 and £6,000 and this was considered excessive. Also in West Africa, but much later in 1847, there was a proposal for a 'Kent and Sussex tower' for James Island in the Gambia. This was to have mounted two 32pdr guns to defend the mouth of the River Gambia, but once again the cost was considered too great and this was never built.[27] This was not the only tower proposed for Africa for, as we have seen, in South Africa in 1837 Colonel Lewis proposed a number of single-gun towers for the

defence of Grahamstown and Fort Beaufort in Eastern Cape
Province, of which the Fort Beaufort tower was the only one built. The
Inspector General of Fortifications, Major-General Mulcaster,
doubted the need for expensive fortifications against an unsophisti-
cated enemy such as the Xhosa tribesmen and would only approve the
construction of the smaller picket towers. Nor would the Board of
Ordnance support a proposal from the Governor of Western Australia
in 1838 for two Martello towers to defend the port of Fremantle.[28]

Across the Atlantic there was something about the air of Canada
which seemed to have an effect on British military engineers. The long,
open border with the United States and the sensitive diplomatic relations with that country throughout the first half of the nineteenth
century caused a number of plans to be put forward for the construction of works to defend Canada. The designs suggested to implement
these plans included some of the most elaborate and expensive
redoubts and towers ever to be conceived by officers of the Royal
Engineers.

As early as 1801 Captain William Fenwick proposed three large
towers for the defence of Citadel Hill in Halifax but, at an estimated
cost of £9,000 each, these proved too expensive to build. His
successor as Commanding Engineer in Halifax, Captain Gustavus
Nicholls, also proposed building a number of towers for the defence
of the port but none were actually built. In 1825 the Carmichael-
Smyth Commission recommended the building of a number of
Martello towers to defend the main routes leading into Canada from
the United States. Among the Commission's proposals were three
towers for Kingston and one to be built on the right bank of the Saint-
Charles River at Quebec.[29]

Treasury opposition in London to most of the commission's
proposals ensured that only limited action was taken and Carmichael-
Smyth's report languished until his proposals were revived again in
1840-41 as a result of deteriorating Anglo-American relations. By
1841 fear of war with the United States resulted in a number of the
proposed towers reaching the design stage with estimates of their cost
being sent to the Board of Ordnance by Lieutenant-Colonel Oldfield,
the commanding Royal Engineer. The towers included one as part of
the defences of the proposed pentagonal redoubt at St. John's and two
on Nun's Island at Chateauguay, all on the Richlieu River in Lower
Canada, and two more on Bois Blanc Island on Lake Huron. Near
Quebec a tower was planned for the right bank of the Saint-Charles
River together with six for Point Levi, and two were proposed to
defend the Niagara border. In addition, six stone towers were to be

sited in a similar fashion to the Martello towers at Quebec to defend Montreal and four for the defence of Kingston.[30]

The tower planned for Chippawa near Niagara and that proposed for the St. John's redoubt were to be standard Martello towers following the design published by Colonel Lewis in the *Professional Papers of the Royal Engineers.*[31] However, the Bois Blanc Island towers, the Niagara border tower planned for Queenston Heights, and the six Point Levi towers were to be square and, unusually, their design closely followed that for the French Napoleonic *Tours Modeles.*[32] The Point Levi towers, larger than those planned for Bois Blanc Island and Queenston Heights, would have represented the culmination of British gun-tower design had they ever been built. They were actually designed to be forts and would have been very large with a planned diameter of 141ft (43.38m) across the ditch and a height of 42ft (12.9m) to the base of an unusual turret where the heavy gun was to be mounted. The tower was to have been sited within a ditch with two caponiers providing access to counterscarp casemates which would have provided accommodation for the garrison of 130 officers and men. The armament planned for the tower was one heavy 24pdr gun on the turret, four 'Miller' brass 24pdr howitzers inside the tower and four more in the counterscarp casemates to provide reverse fire.

These Canadian towers were defeated by their high estimated cost of construction and by the developing debate as to whether Britain or the colony should bear the burden of the cost of the latter's defence. Linked to these factors was an additional one - that of gradually improving relations with the United States after the conclusion of the 'Oregon crisis' in 1846 by the agreed settlement of the border between Canada and the United States. As a result, the plans for these sophisticated towers were destined to remain in the files of the Board of Ordnance unexecuted.

So it is clear that the popularity of gun-towers as a form of permanent defence both in Britain and abroad continued unabated until the middle of the nineteenth century. As the century progressed the designs of the towers became larger and more elaborate, and increasingly more expensive. The more expensive the towers became the more frequently they fell foul of Treasury parsimony. Despite numerous war scares the baleful influence of the Treasury remained paramount and the vast majority of the proposals to build towers never left the drawing board. In the nineteenth century the Board of Ordnance and the Commanding Engineers were just as much subject to financial constraint as the Ministry of Defence is today.

CHAPTER 11

The American Towers

No study of Martello towers could really be complete without a description of a number of similar towers built in the United States. The years between 1800 and 1870 saw the planning and construction of a number of gun-towers modelled, fairly loosely, on the British towers built in Canada. It is these towers which are today known to Americans as 'Martello' towers, although only three of those remaining, or of which we have detailed descriptions, appear to have resembled the British towers reasonably closely. It is probable that the design of these towers was influenced by the design of the Prince of Wales Tower at Halifax, but it is not certain to what extent the first two towers to be built in the United States followed the British design as neither the towers nor their plans exist today.

Deteriorating relations with Great Britain during the Revolutionary War with France and the subsequent Napoleonic Wars led to the construction of the first tower, sited on Dumplings Rocks in Narragansett Bay, Rhode Island. This was a masonry tower constructed between 1800 and 1802 and was elliptical in shape and designed to mount eight guns, four on the terreplein firing *en barbette* and four mounted in casemates. Although this was the earliest American tower it was never completed but was eventually demol-

Late nineteenth-century photograph of the tower on Tybee Island, Savannah, Georgia.
[Fortification Map File, Dr 68, Sheet 30, Office of the Chief of Engineers, Record Group 77, US National Archives]

ished in 1898 to make way for Fort Wetherill. Seven years later a second tower was built as part of the defences of Fort Warburton on the site of the present Fort Washington in Maryland. Fort Warburton was one of the 'First System' of harbour defences built between 1790 and 1812 and these forts, all earthworks, were protected from attack from the rear by infantry redoubts or blockhouses made of wood or brick.

At Fort Warburton this more substantial octagonal tower was built in 1809 on raised ground behind the fort. The tower had a short life and, although the date of its demolition is uncertain, it is probable that it was destroyed in 1814 when Fort Warburton was evacuated and destroyed by its drunken commander when a British naval squadron under the command of Captain James Gordon, RN sailed up the Potomac.[1] Between 1814 and 1824 the new Fort Washington was built on the site of the destroyed structure and a plan of the fort dated 1839 shows Martello towers in each of the two bastions.[2] It would appear that these towers were part of a plan for the rebuilding of the fort which was never implemented as there is no sign of these towers in the fort as it is today. However, the proposal to add the towers to Fort Washington is an indication that Martello towers were much in the minds of the US Army engineers at this time.

The War of 1812 brought about a rapid expansion in the number of fortifications along the coastline of the United States and this 'Second System' included three more gun-towers. The first of these, the Walbach Tower, was erected close to Fort Constitution at Portsmouth, New Hampshire, to prevent an enemy from landing on the southern flank of the fort, and was named after its builder John Walbach. A number of other American coastal forts were defended on the landward side by wooden blockhouses, but the Walbach Tower was a circular brick tower, not as tall as the British Martello towers, being only 20ft (6.15m) high, and with three embrasures in the wall for guns. The armament was one 32pdr gun mounted *en barbette* on top, and three 4pdr guns, one firing through each embrasure and, in this respect, the design appears to indicate the influence of the Canadian towers at Halifax, although the actual design of the tower did not really resemble that of these towers. After the end of the war in 1815 the tower was converted into a powder magazine and then some years later, when it had ceased to be used, it was allowed to fall into ruin.[3]

The other two towers closest in design to the British towers were one on Tybee Island near Savannah, Georgia and another on James Island in the harbour of Charleston, South Carolina. Both were

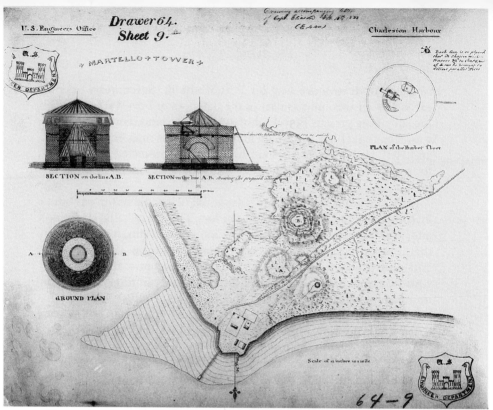

Plan and section of a tower built on James Island to defend Charleston Harbour. [Fortification Map File, Dr 64, Sheet 9, Records of the Office of Chief of Engineers, Record Group 77, US National Archives]

circular with massive, loopholed walls and their dimensions were similar. The Tybee Island tower, completed in 1814-15, was taller than the Charleston tower being 50ft (15m) high. The thickness of the wall was 10ft (3m). The upper gun-platform, which was designed for one gun, was supported by a hollow brick column, as in the Halifax towers, and there was an overhanging wooden, machicolated gallery projecting from the parapet. Originally the tower had had a single door which, like the British towers, was at first-floor level, but a second on the ground floor was added at a later date. During the American Civil War the tower was garrisoned first by Confederate troops and was then captured in 1861 by Union forces. At the end of the war Tybee Island tower was abandoned and then lay derelict until it was eventually demolished at the end of the century when Fort Screven, an Endicott Board fortification, was constructed on the island.

The James Island tower was described as a Martello tower on drawings produced by the US Army Office of Engineers, dated February 1833. These show proposed alterations to the original plan, reducing its height by lowering the parapet and providing an internal bomb-proof arch. The entrance was through the parapet wall and approached by an external ladder.[4] It is unlikely that these alterations were ever carried out since the tower still had a wooden interior when it caught fire in May 1859 and was partially destroyed.[5]

An hexagonal tower, Tower Dupre, was built in 1829-30 on the right bank of Bayou Dupre in Louisiana, at the western end of Lake Borgne. The role of the tower was to defend an approach to New Orleans which had been used by British forces when they made their abortive attack on the city in 1815. Initially the American government did not put a high priority on this particular defensive work as plans for the tower's construction were drawn up in 1821 but work did not actually start on the tower and its adjacent battery until 1829. However, it then proceeded rapidly and the tower was completed in 1830 at a reported cost of $16,677. Tower Dupre was a masonry tower the wall of which was 30ft (9.2m) high and 6ft (1.8m) thick at the base. As originally constructed, it was a three-storey tower with loopholes at ground-floor level and embrasures for an armament of six carronades on the upper floors.[6] In the years following its completion the tower suffered damage from hurricanes, a flood and neglect and in 1847 the decision was taken to reduce the tower in height to two storeys and to fit a conical slate roof.

A report to the Secretary of War by the Board of Engineers of the US Army in 1851 showed that the peacetime garrison was ten men which was to be increased to thirty-six in time of war, or as the report described it, 'siege', and the armament comprised four 24pdr guns, two 8in heavy howitzers and one 10in mortar.[7] Tower Dupre continued to be garrisoned during the Civil War and, like the Tybee Island tower, was abandoned after the war ended. The conversion of Bayou Dupre into a canal in 1873-74 resulted in the tower's standing in water 33yd (30m) from the present shore of Lake Borgne where it still exists, the only tower in any way resembling a Martello tower surviving in the United States today.

There is evidence in the reports of the House of Representatives from 1840 and 1851 that there were plans to build another tower, this time in Alabama. This was to have been built at Pass au Heron, Grant

Tower Dupre, Louisiana; also known as Castle Martello, this now stands in water at the edge of Lake Borgne. [Fortification Map File, Dr 86, Sheet 15-17, Records of the Office of the Chief Engineer, Record Group 77, US National Archives]

Pass, on the shores of Mobile Bay. It would have been similar to Tower Dupre, also with a garrison of ten increasing to a war establishment of thirty-six but with a larger armament, comprising six 24pdr guns, two 18pdr guns, two 12pdr guns and two 8in heavy howitzers. The tower at Pass au Heron was never built but this tower and Tower Dupre were the only ones whose construction was shown as authorized as part of the third harbour-defence programme. In the reports of 1840 and 1851 Tower Dupre is shown as completed but the tower at Pass au Heron remained simply as a proposal.[8]

While the designs of the first three American towers appear to have been based generally on the British Martello tower concept, the designs of three later examples more closely resemble those of the French *Tours Modeles*. These towers probably reflect a change in military fashion away from the successful post-Napoleonic British methods of fortification to a desire to emulate the newly fashionable French methods of Napoleon III's military architects. This French influence in the Corps of Engineers resulted from the appointment to the US Army Board of Engineers of the French engineer officer Brigadier-General Simon Bernard who had served under Napoleon. In 1816 a board of officers was set up under General Bernard and which included Lieutenant-Colonel Joseph G. Totten as one of its members. Totten was later to be Chief of Army Engineers for twenty-six years from 1838 to 1864. The board was convened to consider the defence of the coastline of the United States and for its first five years the members travelled widely, inspecting existing fortifications and assessing the defensive requirements of the major ports and water-ways. By 1821 the board produced its first report which, together with subsequent ones, was to lead to the construction of the famous 'Third System' of American coastal fortifications.

The three later towers were actually small forts and were brick structures, much larger than Martello towers, but, like them, designed for coastal defence. Construction of the first of these towers, at Proctor's Landing on the south side of Lake Borgne, began in 1856; it was designed as a three-storey tower surrounded by a double moat and built to support a battery. The total armament, given in the 1851 report, was to have been considerable. It was shown as twelve 32pdr guns, three 18pdr guns, three 12pdr guns, eight 'Flank' howitzers and eleven 8in heavy howitzers. Work on the tower continued until 1860, and although both the the the tower and the battery were unfinished when the Civil War started both were garrisoned by the Confederate Army until 1863 when the area was evacuated after the fall of New Orleans. The tower was then abandoned, falling into disrepair but the remains may still be seen today.

By the 1820s Key West, a small island at the end of the Florida Keys, the southernmost part of Florida and of the United States, had become the largest town and port in the state and, because of its strategic location, of increasing interest to the US Navy. Among the Bernard board's recommendations were proposals for the construction of defence works at Key West and on the Dry Tortugas, a group of small islands some seventy miles south of Key West. There were considerable delays in the implementation of these proposals, but the reports of 1840 and 1851 refer to the proposed defence work at Key West which was to be a large, two-tiered, casemated fort, eventually named Fort Zachary Taylor, but the reports make no mention of any towers. The construction of Fort Taylor was prolonged, taking from 1845 to 1861, and it was during the building of it that towers for Key West were first suggested. It was at this time that the engineer-in-charge, Captain George Dutton, wrote to the Chief of Engineers with the suggestion that five Martello towers should be built to improve the defences of the fort. Initially this recommendation was ignored by Washington.

At the start of the Civil War in 1861 Fort Taylor was occupied by Union forces and Key West became the only port in the South to be held by the Union and, as such, was a vital point in the Union blockade of the Confederate States. It was the strategic importance of Key West which was the ultimate spur in the construction of the final

two 'Martello' towers to be built in America. The need to reinforce Fort Taylor resulted in Captain Dutton's proposal for Martello towers being reconsidered and the new engineer-in-charge, Captain Edward B. Hunt, was instructed by Army headquarters in Washington to improve the defences by building two towers to secure the landward approaches to Fort Taylor.

The original plan was to have been for simple, square towers, each with a ditch and glacis, to prevent a landing on the beaches in the rear of the fort, but this plan was amended in 1862 by the addition of a large, two-tiered, casemate battery, a

The East Martello Tower, Key West, Florida. [Author's photograph]

counterscarp gallery, a caponier and a wet ditch. The towers themselves were to be 56ft (17m) square and 36ft (11m) high with machicolation on each wall and two lines of tall, narrow, musketry loopholes. The walls were 8ft 4in (2.56m) thick facing the sea and 5ft 4in (1.64m) thick on the land side; entrance to the tower was by means of a small drawbridge at first- floor level connecting with the top of the counterscarp gallery. The towers each had a central, hollow, brick pillar to support the gun-platform, and within the pillar was a cast-iron spiral staircase providing access to all floors and the platform. The floors of the towers were reinforced with cast-iron girders and supported by groined vaulting.[9]

The armament of the towers was planned to be four 100pdr rifled Parrott guns while the two-tiered casemate battery was to have had fourteen 10in Rodman smooth-bore guns in the lower tier and on the parapet. In fact, work ceased on the towers in 1866 at the end of the Civil War, by which time only the first level of the casemate battery had been completed, and no armament was ever mounted in either of the towers.[10]

During the war a narrow-gauge railway was built running from Fort Taylor along the south shore of Key West to the two towers, then known as Towers 1 and 2. The railway was used to move supplies and building materials and was the first one to operate in Key West until the arrival of Flagler's Florida East Coast Railroad linking Miami with Key West in 1912. Although work on the towers ended in 1866 construction was not officially abandoned until 1873. After that, the West Martello Tower (Tower 1) was used as a target for the guns of Fort Taylor and was partially demolished as a result. Further destruction occurred when local people pilfered the bricks and today only a

The gun platform of the East Martello Tower, showing two of the four gun positions. [Author's photograph]

small portion of the eastern wall still exists as part of the garden of the Key West Garden Society. The East Martello Tower (Tower 2) was used by the US Army for training purposes and accommodation up to 1950 when it was handed over by the Department of Defense to the Key West Art and Historical Society and is now an art gallery and museum.

Five further towers were built in the United States between 1820 and 1835. These were not coastal defence towers but formed part of two defensible barrack; one, Fort Snelling near Minneapolis and the second, Jackson Barracks, in New Orleans. Fort Snelling was built to house troops defending the newly opened lands close to the Canadian border. It was situated on the bank of the Mississippi river, diamond-shaped and surrounded by a high stone wall. On the western side a large, loopholed, circular stone tower acted as a keep, while at intervals along the rest of the wall there were three small hexagonal bastions. Fort Snelling is now an historic site and the tower is open to the public.

In New Orleans a defensible barracks was built on the east bank of the Mississippi river and completed in 1835. The barracks were designed to act as a supply base and to provide accommodation for the troops manning the four forts defending New Orleans. Named Jackson Barracks after the Civil War, it had circular towers, one at each corner of the wall. These towers resembled the later Branch Ditch towers built at Kingston in Canada. Each tower had musketry loopholes and a number of embrasures in the parapet for light guns. In 1912 the levee collapsed destroying the two towers and the section of the wall facing the river, and now only the towers on the landward side remain. Today the barracks house the headquarters of the Louisiana National Guard and the powder magazine has been converted into the Louisiana Military History and State Weapons Museum.

Conclusion

The construction of masonry gun-towers by British military engineers covered a period of eighty years from 1780 to 1860. Gun-towers were a standard element in the portfolio of the military engineer in the seventeenth and the eighteenth century and many were built in the Mediterranean by Spanish and Italian engineers; but it was the development of these towers by British engineers in the early nineteenth century which resulted in the simple, elegant, and extremely practical design which is today known as the Martello tower. Although the construction of the English towers did not start until 1805, towers had already been built on Minorca and Trinidad, and in 1803 work had started on similar towers in Ireland. Other towers had been completed even earlier on Jersey and Guernsey, at Halifax in Canada, and also at Cape Town. These towers were the forerunners of the extensive chain of English towers built between 1805 and 1810.

Situated for the most part to defend the coastline from attack from the sea and usually sited to provide each other with mutual fire-support, these towers would have been difficult to destroy. The majority provided the first line of defence for the most vulnerable part of the English coast, that nearest to the ancient enemy France. Others were to be found in Ireland and throughout the British Empire, and a number were used as land defences to protect the outworks of citadels and colonial frontiers. This was the case in Quebec, Delhi and on the frontier of the Eastern Cape Province in South Africa, where Martello towers provided a cheap and effective form of permanent fortification.

The cost of construction of the English towers was about £350,000, including the cost of the three circular redoubts, and to this sum should be added a further £150,000 for the towers in Ireland. The total spent in providing these defences exceeded £500,000, an enormous sum at the time when it is considered that the total expenditure of the British government in 1811 was only £82 million. This vast expenditure on fixed defences, exceeded only by the cost of the defences built around the English naval bases in the 1860s, can probably be equated with the cost of the *Trident* nuclear missile system in our time and demonstrates the high cost of military deterrence.

These towers were designed and built by a small number of talented Royal Engineer officers whose influence is to be found wherever Martello towers were built. The names Twiss, Fisher, D'Arcy, Birch,

Bridges, Bryce, Ford, Pasley, Lewis and Whitmore feature again and again when the origins of the towers are studied. Twiss, Ford and Whitmore were responsible for the towers in England, and D'Arcy, Birch and Pasley, among others, for those on Minorca. Fisher, Birch and D'Arcy were involved in designing and building the Irish towers, while Bryce produced the original design for the Leith tower and subsequently supervised the building of towers in Sicily. Bridges built towers at Cape Town and in Ceylon, and Lewis was responsible for the later towers on the Channel Islands and in South Africa. Pasley became the first commandant of the School of Military Engineering at Chatham and wrote a noted textbook on the theory of fortification which included a chapter on the principles to be followed when designing Martello towers. Ten years later Lewis wrote a shorter monograph on gun-towers which was published in the *Professional Papers of the Royal Engineers*. This laid down a series of designs which were to become the standard patterns for all such towers.

The essential characteristics of the Martello tower were its circular or elliptical shape, massive wall and entrance through a doorway at first-floor level. In the larger towers there was a massive central pillar which supported a bomb-proof arch. However, many later towers were more sophisticated with glacis, counterscarp galleries and caponiers. For fifty years Martello towers provided an effective and frequently economic form of coastal defence and protection for harbours; but it was the advent in the 1860s of modern, rifled artillery and iron-clad warships, together with changing political alliances, which brought about their demise. By 1870 the towers were obselete as defensive works and were replaced instead by large, concealed, earthwork forts mounting large-calibre, rifled, muzzle-loading guns which were later replaced by breech-loading guns.

Although some Martello towers remained the responsibility of the War Office until the end of the nineteenth century, many were sold soon after the end of the Napoleonic Wars in 1815, or used by the Coast Blockade and its successor the Coastguard. However, the reduction in duty on many imported goods in the 1850s made smuggling no longer profitable and then the fate of most of the remaining towers was that of abandonment and dereliction. In the Second World War a number of shoreline towers were adapted to defend the beaches with modern weapons against an enemy who, once again, never came. After the war a few remained in service as Coastguard stations and some were converted into residences or holiday homes.

More than 200 Martello towers were built around the world by the British government between 1796 and 1857. The towers defended the coastline, harbours and islands of the United Kingdom and harbours and anchorages - and even cities - throughout the world. Many of these towers still stand today, splendid examples of military engineering. They remain part of our heritage and a reminder of a period in our history when Britain stood alone against the might of Napoleonic France.

Annex A

Martello Towers Remaining in Great Britain, Ireland and the Channel Islands

Tower	Location	Date	Diameter (ft)	Height (ft)	Shape	Original armament	Comments
ENGLAND							
1	Wear Bay Road, East Cliff, Folkestone, Kent	1805-08	48	33	ellip[1]	1x24pdr 1x5$^{1}/_{2}$in howitzer	now a house
2	Wear Bay Road, East Cliff, Folkestone, Kent	1805-08	48	33	ellip	1x24pdr 1x5$^{1}/_{2}$in howitzer	now a house
3	Wear Bay Road, East Cliff, Folkestone, Kent	1805-08	48	33	ellip	1x24pdr 1x5$^{1}/_{2}$in howitzer	now a tourist information centre
4	The Leas, Folkestone, Kent	1805-08	48	33	ellip	1x24pdr 1x5$^{1}/_{2}$in howitzer	located in garden of a house; derelict
5	Folkestone School for Girls, Coolinge Lane, Folkestone, Kent	1805-08	48	33	ellip	1x24pdr 1x5$^{1}/_{2}$in howitzer	in grounds of the Girls School
6	Shorncliffe Army camp, Folkestone, Kent	1805-08	48	33	ellip	1x24pdr 1x5$^{1}/_{2}$in howitzer	edge of the camp boundary, access from Military Road; derelict
7	Shorncliffe Army camp, Folkestone, Kent	1805-08	48	33	ellip	1x24pdr 1x5$^{1}/_{2}$in howitzer	within the Army camp; derelict
8	Hospital Road, Shorncliffe, Folkestone, Kent	1805-08	48	33	ellip	1x24pdr 1x5$^{1}/_{2}$in howitzer	now a house
9	Shorncliffe, Folkestone, Kent	1805-08	48	33	ellip	1x24pdr 1x5$^{1}/_{2}$in howitzer	approached through Military Cemetery; derelict

Tower	Location	Date	Diameter (ft)	Height (ft)	Shape	Original armament	Comments
13	West Parade, Hythe, Kent	1805-08	48	33	ellip	1x24pdr	now a house
14	Hythe Beach, Hythe, Kent	1805-08	48	33	ellip	1x24pdr	inside Army firing range
15	Hythe Beach, Hythe, Kent	1805-08	48	33	ellip	1x24pdr	inside Army firing range
19	beach between Hythe and Dymchurch, Kent	1805-08	48	33	ellip	1x24pdr	inside Army firing range; now partially demolished
23	eastern outskirts of Dymchurch, Kent	1805-08	48	33	ellip	1x24pdr	now a house
24	centre of village, Dymchurch, Kent	1805-08	48	33	ellip	1x24pdr	owned by English Heritage; open to the public
25	beach car park, Dymchurch, Kent	1805-08	48	33	ellip	1x24pdr	maintained by the District Council
28	caravan park, Rye Harbour, East Sussex	1805-08	48	33	ellip	1x24pdr	derelict
30	Winchelsea Road, Rye, East Sussex	1805-08	48	33	ellip	1x24pdr	previously a house, now surrounded by a scrap yard
55	Normans Bay, nr Bexhill, East Sussex	1805-08	48	33	ellip	1x24pdr	disused but recently up for sale with permission for conversion to a house
60	Leyland Road, Pevensey Bay, East Sussex	1805-08	48	33	ellip	1x24pdr	now a house
61	Martello Square, Millward Road, Pevensey Bay, East Sussex	1805-08	48	33	ellip	1x24pdr	previously a house, now unoccupied
64	Crumbles, Eastbourne, East Sussex	1805-08	48	33	ellip	1x24pdr	stands on beach; disused

Tower	Location	Date	Diameter (ft)	Height (ft)	Shape	Original armament	Comments
66	Langney Point, Eastbourne, East Sussex	1805-08	48	33	ellip	1x24pdr	previously used by HM Coastguard; now empty
73	King Edwards Parade, Eastbourne, East Sussex	1805-08	48	33	ellip	1x24pdr	open to the public as a museum
74	The Esplanade, Seaford, East Sussex	1810	48	33	ellip	1x24pdr	now a museum; open to the public
A	Point Clear, St. Osyth, Essex	1809-12	55	33	cam	1x24pdr 2x24pdr carronades	now the East Essex Aviation Museum
C	Haven Caravan Park, Seawick Sands, Essex	1809-12	55	33	cam	1x24pdr 2x24pdr carronades	disused
D	Clacton golf course, Jaywick Sands, Clacton- on-Sea, Essex	1809-12	55	33	cam	1x24pdr 2x5^{1}/$_{2}$in howitzers	disused
E	Hastings Avenue, Clacton-on-Sea, Essex	1809-12	55	33	cam	1x24pdr 2x5^{1}/$_{2}$in howitzers	previously used as a water tower, now disused
F	Marine Parade West, Clacton-on-Sea, Essex	1809-12	55	33	cam	1x24pdr 2x5^{1}/$_{2}$in howitzers	now used by Sea Scouts
K	Martello Caravan Park, Walton-on-the-Naze, Essex	1809-12	55	33	cam	1x24pdr 2x5^{1}/$_{2}$in howitzers	disused
L	Police Training Centre, Shotley Gate, Suffolk	1809-12	55	33	cam	1x24pdrs 2x24pdr carronades	previously used as a water tower and naval signal station
M	Shotley Gate Marina, Shotley Gate, Suffolk	1809-12	55	33	cam	1x24pdr 2x24pdr carronades	previously used as a water tower
P	Landguard Road, Felixstowe, Suffolk	1809-12	55	33	cam	1x24pdr 2x5^{1}/$_{2}$in howitzers	previously used by HM Coastguard; now owned by the DistrictCouncil

Tower	Location	Date	Diameter (ft)	Height (ft)	Shape	Original armament	Comments
Q	South Hill, Felixstowe, Suffolk	1809-12	55	33	cam	1x24pdr 2x5¹/₂in howitzers	now a house
T	Felixstowe golf course, Felixstowe, Suffolk	1809-12	55	33	cam	1x24pdr 2x24pdr carronades	now a golf club store
U	Felixstowe Ferry, Felixstowe, Suffolk	1809-12	55	33	cam	1x24pdr 2x5¹/₂in howitzers	being reconverted to a house
W	Bawdsey Cliffs, Bawdsey, Suffolk	1809-12	55	33	cam	1x24pdr 2x5¹/₂in howitzers	now a house
Y	Bawdsey, Suffolk	1809-12	55	33	cam	1x24pdr 2x24pdr carronades	derelict
Z	Alderton, Suffolk	1809-12	55	33	cam	1x24pdr 2x24pdr carronades	derelict
AA	Shingle Street, Suffolk	1809-12	55	33	cam	1x24pdr 2x24pdr carronades	now a house
CC	Slaughden, Aldeburgh, Suffolk	1809-12	77	40	quatrefoil	4x24pdrs	now owned by Landmark Trust
Grain Tower	Isle of Grain, Kent	1855	63	42	oval	1x56pdr 2x32pdr	disused and derelict
WALES							
N.E. Martello Tower	Pembroke Dock Pembrokeshire	1848-51	76	49	oval	3x32pdr 3x12pdr howitzers	now tourist information centre
S.W. Martello Tower	Pembroke Dock	1848-51	52	42	square	1x32pdr 4x12pdr howitzers	disused
SCOTLAND							
Leith Tower	Leith Harbour, Edinburgh	1810-44	80	45	circ	3x32pdrs	now part of Leith Harbour breakwater; no armament ever mounted

Tower	Location	Date	Diameter (ft)	Height (ft)	Shape	Original armament	Comments
Hackness Tower	Hackness, Hoy, Orkney Scotland;	1812-15	47	33	ellip	1x24pdr	owned by Historic Scotland open to the public
Crockness Tower	Crockness, Hoy, Orkney	1812-15	47	33	ellip	1x24pdr	disused
GUERNSEY							
Fort Hommet	Vazon Bay	1804-05	34	17	circ	1x24pdr carronade	disused
Fort Saumarez	Rocquaine Bay	1804-05	34	17	circ	1x24pdr carronade	privately owned; now derelict but with a WW II German OP built on top
Fort Grey	Rocquaine Bay	1804-05	36	26	circ	1x24pdr carronade	now maritime museum
Brehon Tower	off St. Peter Port	1854-56	85	34	oval	3x68pdr 2x8in shell guns	derelict
JERSEY							
Icho Tower	Banc du Violet, St. Clements Bay	1808-10	43	39	circ	1x24pdr	maintained by the Public Services Dept
Portelet Tower	Ile au Guerdain, Portelet Bay	1808-10	27	17	circ	1x18pdr carronade	maintained by the Public Services Dept
La Tour de Vinde	Noirmont Point	1808-10	26	23	circ	1x18pdr	maintained by Harbour & Airport Committee
Kempt Tower	St. Ouens Bay	1834	54	35	cam	3x24pdr	now National Trust for Jersey Interpretation Centre
La Collette Tower	Pointe des Pas, St Helier	1834	56	33	cam	3x24pdr	maintained by the Public Services Dept
Lewis Tower	St. Ouens Bay	1835	39	33	circ	1x24pdr	maintained by the Public Services Dept

Tower	Location	Date	Diameter (ft)	Height (ft)	Shape	Original armament	Comments
Victoria Tower	Gorey	1837	32	33	circ	1x24pdr	owned by National Trust for Jersey

IRELAND

Dublin North

1	Sutton Creek	1804-06	38	24	circ	1x24pdr	now a house
2	Howth	1804-06	40	24	circ	1x24pdr	disused
3	Irelands Eye Island	1804-06	52	24	circ	2x24pdr	disused
4	Carrick Hill, Portmarnock	1804-06	38	24	circ	1x24pdr	now a house
5	Robswall, Malahide	1804-06	40	24	circ	1x24pdr	now a house
6	Balcarrick	1804-06	35	24	circ	1x24pdr	derelict
7	Portrane	1804-06	40	24	circ	1x24pdr	now a house
8	Rush	1804-06	38	24	circ	1x24pdr	disused
9	Drummanagh	1804-06	40	24	circ	1x24pdr	derelict
10	Shennicks Island	1804-06	38	24	circ	1x24pdr	derelict
11	Skerries	1804-06	38	24	circ	1x24pdr	disused
12	Balbriggan	1804-06	38	24	circ	1x24pdr	derelict

Dublin South

2	Bray Point	1804-06	38	24	circ	1x18pdr	
6	Loughlinstown River	1804-06	38	24	circ	1x18pdr	now a house
7	Tara Hill, Killiney	1804-06	40	24	circ	1x18pdr	
9	Dalkey Island	1804-06	45	33	circ	2x24pdr	derelict
10	Bullock	1804-06	40	24	circ	1x18pdr	now part of new housing estate
11	Sandycove	1804-06	38	24	circ	1x18pdr	now James Joyce Museum
14	Seapoint	1804-06	38	24	circ	1x18pdr	
15	Seafort Parade, Williamstown	1804-06	45	24	circ	2x18pdr	disused
16	Sandymount	1804-06	45	24	circ	2x18pdr	previously used as cafe

Wexford

Baginbun Tower	Baginbun Head, Fethard-on-Sea, Co. Wexford	1805-06	37	33	circ	1x24pdr carronade	now a house
1	Duncannon, Co. Wexford	1814-15	48	33	ellip	1x24pdr 1x5½in howitzer	disused
2	Duncannon, Co. Wexford	1814-15	48	33	ellip	1x24pdr 1x5½in howitzer	now a house

Cork

Manning Tower	Marino Point, Great Island, Cork Harbour	1813-15	40	37	circ	1x24pdr	disused

Tower	Location	Date	Diameter (ft)	Height (ft)	Shape	Original armament	Comments
Belvelly Tower	Belvelly, Great Island, Cork Harbour	1813-15	40	37	circ	1x24pdr	disused
Rossleague Tower	Rossleague, Great island, Cork Harbour	1813-15	40	37	circ	1x24pdr	disused
Ringaskiddy Tower	Ringaskiddy, Co. Cork	1813-15	51	40	oval	2x24pdrs	designed for two guns but only one mounted
Haulbowline Tower	Haulbowline Island, Cork Harbour	1813-15	50	37	circ	1x24pdr	used by Irish Naval Service
Cloughlan Tower	Bere Island, Co. Cork	1804-05	38	28	circ	1x24pdr	derelict
Ardagh Tower	Bere Island, Co. Cork	1804-05	n.a.	n.a.	circ	1x24pdr	derelict
Garinish Tower	Garinish Island, Glenarriff, Co .Cork	1804-06	37	34	circ	1x8in howitzer	maintained by Irish Board of Works

Galway

Tower	Location	Date	Diameter (ft)	Height (ft)	Shape	Original armament	Comments
Rossaveel Tower	Cashla Bay, Costelloe, Co. Galway	1810-12	45	33	ellip	1x24pdr 1x8in howitzer	derelict
Meelick Tower	Meelick, Co. Galway	1810-12	55	33	cam	1x24pdr 2x5½in howitzers	derelict

Clare

Tower	Location	Date	Diameter (ft)	Height (ft)	Shape	Original armament	Comments
Aughinish Tower	nr Kinvara, Co. Clare	1810-12	55	33	cam	1x24pdr 2x5½in howitzers	derelict
Finnavarra Tower	nr Kinvara, Co. Clare	1810-12	55	33	cam	1x24pdrs 2x5½in howitzers	derelict

Donegal

Tower	Location	Date	Diameter (ft)	Height (ft)	Shape	Original armament	Comments
Knockalla Fort	nr Ballymastocker Bay, Lough Swilly, Donegal	1810-12	65	n.a.	cam	1x24pdr 1x5½in howitzer	now a holiday home
Muckamish Fort	Muckamish Point, Lough Swilly, Donegal	1810-12	52	n.a.	circ	2x24pdr	now a holiday home

Tower	Location	Date	Diameter (ft)	Height (ft)	Shape	Original armament	Comments
Greencastle Fort	Greencastle, Lough Foyle, Donegal	1812-15	65	48	circ	2x 24pdr carronades	now part of an hotel
Londonderry							
Magilligan Tower	Magilligan Point, Co. Londonderry	1812-15	53	36	circ	2x24pdr	maintained by Department of Environment
Offaly							
Fanesker Tower	Banagher, Co. Offaly	1810-12	48	33	ellip	1x24pdr	disused

Note 1. See sectional drawings on p.19

Annex B

Smooth-bore Guns, Howitzers and Mortars in Use in the British Army between 1795 and 1825

Type	Weight (cwt)	Length (ft)	Bore (in)	Range (yd at 5 degrees elevation)	Comments
Guns:					
68pdr	60	8.00	8.05	1,620	
	50	6.67	8.05	1,480	
32pdr	63	9.58	6.41	1,950	
	56	9.50	6.41	1,950	
	48	8.00	6.41	1,740	
24pdr	50	9.50	5.82	1,850	
	48	9.00	5.82	1,850	
	40	7.50	5.82	1,800	
	33	6.50	5.82	1,560	
18pdr	42	9.00	5.29	1,780	
	38	8.00	5.29	1,730	
12pdr	42	9.00	4.62	1,700	
	29	7.50	4.62	1,650	
9pdr	26	7.50	4.20	1,600	
6pdr	17	6.00	3.67	1,520	
Shell guns (c.1850):					
10in	84	9.33	10.60	1,700	
8in	65	9.00	8.05	1,700	

Type	Weight (cwt)	Length (ft)	Bore (in)	Range (yd at 5 degrees elevation)	Comments
Carronades:					
68pdr	36	5.33	8.05	1,420	
	29	4.00	8.05		
42pdr	22	4.50	6.84	1,350	
32pdr	17	4.00	6.25	1,260	
24pdr	13	3.75	5.68	1,150	
18pdr	10	3.33	5.16	1,100	
12pdr	6	2.67	4.52	1,000	
Howitzers:					
8in brass obselete	12³/₄	3.08	n.a.	1,700	range at 12 deg; weight of shell 46lb; by 1815
12pdr brass	6¹/₂	3.75	4.58	1,200	range at 12 deg; weight of shell 11lb; introduced into service in 1822
5¹/₂in	9¹/₂	2.67	5.66	1,700	range at 12 deg; weight of shell 16lb;
51/2in light brass	4	2.25	5.66	1,350	range at 12 deg; weight of shell 16lb
51/2in heavy iron	16	3.50	5.66	1,900	range at 9 deg; weight of shell 16lb
Mortars:					
13in land	37³/₄	3.67	13.00	690-2,700	range at 45 deg; weight of shell 200lb
10in land	42	3.75	10.00	680-2,500	range at 45 deg; weight of shell 93lb
8in land	8	1.83	8.00	500-1,700	range at 45 deg; weight of shell 46lb
coehorn	96lb	1.17	4.52	800	range at 45 deg; weight of shell 9lb

Notes

Archive sources:

IOL	India Office Library
MAD	Military Archives, Dublin
NAM	National Army Museum
NLI	National Library of Ireland
OIOC	British Library Oriental and India Office Collection
PRO	Public Record Office
PRONI	Public Record Office Northern Ireland
SOC JER	Société Jersiaise

Introduction

1. PRO WO 30/73
2. PRO WO 1/783, pp.297-99

Chapter 1

1. Pegden, Brian K., 'The Purchase of Bricks for Martello Towers in the Year 1804', *Fort*, Vol.8, 1980
2. Sutcliffe, Sheila, *Martello Towers* (Newton Abbott: David & Charles, 1972), p.78
3. PRO WO 44/53
4. PRO WO 30/62
5. PRO ADM 1/4654, Pro G 233

Chapter 2

1. Quoted in Longmate, Norman, *Island Fortress* (Hutchinson,1991), p.269
2. PRO WO 30/100
3. Ward, S.G.P., 'Defence Works in Britain 1803-05', *Journal of the Society for Army Historical Research*, No.27, 1949
4. PRO WO 1/629
5. Diary of Maj.-Gen. Brown, National Library of Scotland, Ms 3269; quoted in Vine, Paul, *The Royal Military Canal* (Newton Abbott: David & Charles, 1972)
6. Rose, J. Holland and A.M. Broadley, *Dumouriez and the Defence of England* (London: Bodley Head, 1909)

7. PRO WO 55/778
8. PRO WO 1/783
9. PRO WO 55/778
10. Ibid.
11. Pegden, op. cit.
12. PRO WO 55/733
13. PRO WO 1/783

Chapter 3

1. PRO WO 78/5138
2. PRO WO 54/44
3. PRO WO 33/25
4. PRO WO 55/779
5. PRO WO 54/44
6. PRO WO 33/9
7. Sutcliffe, op. cit. p.99 PRO WO 33/25.
9. PRO WO 33/27
10. Haslam, Charlotte, 'Landmarks in Coastal Defence', *Fortress,* No.4, Feb.1990
11. Ward, Ronald, *The Martello Tower, Hythe* (privately published, nd), p.9

Chapter 4

1. Cullen del Castillo, Pedro, *Torre de Gando* (Gran Canaria: Gando, 1980)
2. PRO WO 1/297
3. Ibid.
4. Pasley, Gen. Sir Charles, *A Course of Elementary Fortification* (London,1822)
5. Walsh, Thomas, Capt., 93rd Foot, *Journal of the Late Campaign in Egypt* (London, 1803)
6. PRO WO 1/298
7. PRO WO 55/901
8. PRO WO 1/299
9. Pasley, op. cit., p.483
10. Kerrigan, Paul M., 'Minorca and Ireland, an Architectural Connection: the Martello Towers of Dublin Bay', *Irish Sword,* Vol.15, 1983
11. Fornells de Villalonga, Col. Francisco, *Torres de Defensa y Atalayas de Menorca* (Mahon: Museo Historico Militar de Menorca, 1989)

Chapter 5

1. PRO WO 30/73
2. PRONI T3465/154
3. PRONI T3465/168
4. PRONI T3465/170
5. PRO WO 55/831
6. Ibid.
7. MAD, plan and section of Dalkey Island tower
8. PRO WO 30/73
9. PRO WO 55/831
10. PRO HO 100/120
11. PRO WO 55/831
12. PRO HO 100/120
13. NLI, Kilmainham Papers, Ms 1122 f.327
14. Alcock, Lt Alex., RA, 'Bere Island in Bantry Bay with a Review of its Effective Powers as a Fortified Place', unpublished notebook, 1824 (NAM Archives, Acc. No. 8409-11)
15. PRO WO 55/831
16. PRO WO 46/27
17. PRO WO 55/835
18. PRO WO 46/27
19. PRO WO 55/835
20. PRO WO 55/831
21. Alcock, op. cit.
22. PRO HO 100/120
23. NLI Ms 4707
24. PRO WO 55/833
25. PRO WO 55/836
26. PRO HO 100/132
27. Kerrigan, Paul M., *Castles and Fortifications in Ireland 1485-1945* (Cork: Collins Press, 1995), p.216
28. Ordnance Survey of Ireland, *Memoirs of Ireland*, Vol.38, *Parishes of Co. Donegal I, 1833-1835* (Belfast: Queen's University, Institute of Irish Studies, 1997), p.4
29. Kerrigan, op. cit., p.239
30. Photograph in O'Carroll, Comdt Declan, The Guns of Dunree (Fort Dunree Military Museum, 1988)
31. Ordnance Survey of Ireland, op. cit., p.25
32. PRO MPHH 641
33. Ordnance Survey of Ireland, *Memoirs of Ireland*, Vol.11, *Parishes of Co. Londonderry III, 1831-1835* (Belfast: Queen's University,

Institute of Irish Studies, 1994), p.85
34. Ibid., p.85
35. PRO WO 55/834

Chapter 6

1. PRO WO 46/10
2. PRO WO 30/57
3. SOC JER, Anon., 'The Fortifications of Jersey and Notes on the Militia', manuscript notebook, 1857
4. PRO WO 55/372
5. PRO WO 55/808
6. PRO WO 44/76
7. Ibid.
8. PRO WO 55/818
9. PRO WO 44/274
10. PRO WO 44/277
11. Ibid.
12. Quoted in Fereday, R.R., *Longhope Battery and Towers* (Stromness, Orkney: W.R.Rendell, 1971) (NAM 623-1)
13. Ibid.
14. Ibid.

Chapter 7

1. Saunders, Ivan J., *A History of Martello Towers in the Defence of British North America 1796-1871* (Canada: National Historic Parks Branch, Occasional Papers in Archaeology and History No.15, 1976), pp.20-1
2. PRO MPH 491
3. PRO WO 78/1671 and Saunders, op. cit., pp.22-3
4. PRO WO 78/1671
5. Ibid.
6. PRO WO 44/80
7. PRO WO 44/144
8. PRO CO 42/136
9. Saunders, op. cit., pp.37-8
10. PRO CO 42/136
11. Saunders, op. cit., pp.35-7

Chapter 8

1. PRO WO 1/297
2. PRO WO 55/911
3. Ibid.
4. Capt W.H.Smith, RN, *Memoir Descriptive of the Resources, Inhabitants, and Hydrography of Sicily and Its Islands* (1824)
5. PRO WO 55/911
6. PRO WO 6/57
7. PRO WO 1/728
8. PRO WO 55/911
9. D.W. King, 'A British Officer in the Eastern Adriatic 1812-1815', *Journal of the Society for Army Historical Research,* Vol.58, 1980, pp.30-1
10. 'Korcula' Berislav Kalogjera Split 1995 and Hughes, Quentin, *Military Architecture* (Beaufort,1991), p.151
11. PRO MPH 703, MPH 712
12. PRO WO 44/65
13. PRO WO 1/352
14. Ibid.
15. PRO WO 44/586
16. PRO WO 44/66
17. PRO WO 44/67
18. PRO CO 700, Mauritius 7
19. Ibid.
20. PRO WO 44/65
21. OIOC, 'Notes on the Siege of Delhi' Archibald Galloway (privately pubd, 1847)
22. H.M. Vibart, *Richard Baird Smith, The Leader of the Delhi Heroes* (London: Constable, 1897)
23. OIOC X 1662
24. Quoted in Nicholson, Desmond V., *Heritage Landmarks of Antigua and Barbuda* (Museum of Antigua and Barbuda, nd)
25. *Naval Chronicle,* 'Biographical Memoir of Admiral Sir Charles Knowles, Bt, RN', Vol.II, 1799
26. Nicholson, op. cit.
27. PRO WO 78/2618
28. PRO WO 44/80
29. PRO WO 44/121
30. Ibid.
31. PRO WO 78/808
32. PRO WO 44/121

33. PRO WO 44/9
34. Details from Harris, Dr Edward, 'The Martello Tower at Ferry
    Point, St. Georges' Island, Bermuda', *Mariner's Mirror,* Vol.74,
    No.2, May 1988

Chapter 9

1. PRO WO 55/730
2. Ibid.
3. Ibid.
4. Ibid.
5. PRO WO 44/313
6. PRO WO 44/128
7. MacDougall, Phillip, *The Isle of Grain Defences* (Kent Defence
    Research Group, 1980), pp.7-9
8. Longmate, op. cit., p.336
9. Grimsley, E.J., *The Historical Development of the Martello Towers in
    the Channel Islands* (Guernsey: Sarnian Press, 1988)
10. PRO WO 55/816; MFQ 1298 Pt 2
11. PRO WO 78/473
12. PRO WO 78/470
13. PRO WO 33/7
14. Saunders, op. cit., pp.66-74
15. Ibid., p.65
16. PRO WO 44/5
17. Ibid.
18. Ibid.
19. Davies, Simon, *The Islands of Sydney Harbour* (Sydney: Hale &
    Iremonger, 1984)

Chapter 10

1. PRO WO 30/100
2. PRO HO 100/831
3. PRO WO 55/833
4. Ibid.
5. PRO WO 44/274
6. PRO WO 55/818
7. PRO WO 44/274
8. PRO WO 30/77
9. PRO WO 55/833
10. PRO WO 55/815

11. PRO WO 44/506
12. PRO WO 1/605
13. PRO WO 55/815; WO 55/816; MPHH 679
14. Goodwin, John, 'Granite Towers of St. Mary's, Isles of Scilly', *Cornish Archaeology,* No.32, 1993, pp.135-6
15. PRO MR 1339
16. PRO WO 55/1548/4
17. PRO WO 1/626
18. PRO WO 44/121
19. PRO WO 78/2618
20. PRO WO 44/121
21. Harris, op. cit.
22. PRO WO 44/9
23. Ibid.
24. PRO WO 55/894
25. Ibid.
26. PRO WO 44/499; ADM 140 1229-12249
27. PRO WO 44/5
28. PRO WO 1/432
29. Saunders, op. cit., p.48
30. PRO WO 44/36; WO 44/37; MPHH 688; MPH 902
31. Lewis, Col. George, RE, 'Report on the Application of Forts, Towers and Batteries to Coast Defences and Harbours', *Professional Papers of the Royal Engineers,* Vol.VII, 1844
32. PRO WO 44/37 and MPHH 688; MPH 902

Chapter 11

1. Floyd, Dale E., 'United States Martello Towers', *Fortress,* No.9, May 1991
2. US National Archives, Fort Washington, 117.8-4, Records of the National Park Service, Record Group 79
3. Floyd, op. cit.
4. US National Archives, Martello Tower, Charleston Harbour. Record and Section Drawer 64, Sheet 9, Fortifications Map File, Record Group 77, Records of the Office of the Chief of Engineers (reproduced in Floyd, op. cit.)
5. Floyd, op. cit.
6. Ibid.
7. US Congress, House of Representatives, *Report on Permanent Fortifications* (Washington:1851)
8. Ibid.

9. Jameson, Colin J., *History of East Martello Tower* (Key West, FL:
Key West Art & Historical Society, 1992)
10. Ibid., p.17

Bibliography

Books and Booklets

Anonymous, 'The Fortifications of Jersey and Notes on the Militia', manuscript notebook, 1857 (Société Jersiaise)

Alcock, Lt Alex., RA, 'Bere Island in Bantry Bay with a Review of its Effective Powers as a Fortified Place', unpublished notebook, 1824 (NAM Archives, Acc. No. 8409-11)

Buisseret, David, *The Fortifications of Kingston 1655-1914* (Jamaica: Bolivar Press, 1970)

Coad, J.G., *Dymchurch Martello Tower* (London: English Heritage,1990)

Cullen del Castillo, Pedro, *Torre de Gando* (Gran Canaria: Gando, 1980)

Davies, Simon, *The Islands of Sydney Harbour* (Sydney: Hale & Iremonger, 1984)

Davies, William, *The Coastal Towers of Jersey* (Société Jersiaise,1991)

Enoch, Victor J., *The Martello Towers of Ireland* (Dublin, 1975)

Fereday, R.R., *Longhope Battery and Towers* (Stromness, Orkney: W.R.Rendell, 1971)

Fornells de Villalonga, Col. Francisco, *Torres de Defensa y Atalayas de Menorca* (Mahon: Museo Historico Militar de Menorca, 1989)

Grimsley, E.J., *The Historical Development of the Martello Towers in the Channel Islands* (Guernsey: Sarnian Press, 1988)

Hughes, Quentin, *Military Architecture* (Beaufort,1991)

Hutchinson, Geoff, *Martello Towers, a Brief History* (Hastings,1994)

Jameson, Colin J., *History of East Martello Tower* (Key West, FL: Key West Art & Historical Society, 1992)

Johnston, J. Forde, *Castles and Fortifications of Britain and Ireland* (Dent, 1977)

Kerrigan, Paul M., *Castles and Fortifications in Ireland 1485-1945* (Cork: Collins Press, 1995)

Kirkwall, Viscount, *Four Years in the Ionian Islands* (London, 1864)

Longmate, Norman, *Island Fortress* (Hutchinson,1991)

Lewis, E.R., *Seacoast Fortifications of the United States* (Washington, DC: Smithsonian Institute Press, 1970)

MacDougall, Phillip, *The Isle of Grain Defences* (Kent Defence Research Group, 1980)

Nelson, W.A., *The Dutch Forts of Sri Lanka* (Canongate, 1984)

Nicholson, Desmond V., *Heritage Landmarks of Antigua and Barbuda* (Museum of Antigua and Barbuda, nd)

Ordnance Survey of Ireland, *Memoirs of Ireland,* Vol.11, *Parishes of Co. Londonderry III, 1831-1835* (Belfast: Queen's University, Institute of Irish Studies, 1994)
-, *Memoirs of Ireland,* Vol.38, *Parishes of Co. Donegal I, 1833-1835* (Belfast: Queen's University, Institute of Irish Studies, 1997)

O'Carroll, Comdt Declan, *The Guns of Dunree* (Fort Dunree Military Museum, 1988)

Pasley, Gen. Sir Charles, *A Course of Elementary Fortification* (London, 1822)

Pocock, Tom, *Remember Nelson: The Life of Captain Sir William Hoste, RN* (London: Collins, 1977)

Rose, J. Holland and A.M. Broadley, *Dumouriez and the Defence of England* (London: Bodley Head, 1909)

Saunders, Andrew, *Fortress Britain: Artillery Fortifications in the British Isles and Ireland* (Beaufort, 1989)

Saunders, Ivan J., *A History of Martello Towers in the Defence of British North America 1796-1871* (Canada: National Historic Parks Branch, Occasional Papers in Archaeology and History No.15, 1976)

South Pembrokeshire District Council, *The Fortifications of Milford Haven* (nd)

Sutcliffe, Sheila, *Martello Towers* (Newton Abbott: David & Charles, 1972)

Telling, Dr R.M., *English Martello Towers: a Concise Guide* (Beckenham, Kent: CST Books, 1997).

US Congress, House of Representatives, *Report on Permanent Fortifications* (Washington: 1851)

Vine, Paul, *The Royal Military Canal* (Newton Abbott: David & Charles, 1972)
Ward, Ronald, *The Martello Tower, Hythe* (Privately published, nd)

Articles

Brandreth, Capt., RE, 'Notes on the Island of Ascension', *Professional Papers of the Royal Engineers,* Vol.IV

Cross, Ian, 'Blockhouses and Towers in South Africa', *Soldiers of the Queen*

(Journal of the Victorian Military Society), Nos. 64, 65 and 66

Floyd, Dale E., 'United States Martello Towers', *Fortress,* No.9, May 1991

Goodwin, John, 'Granite Towers of St. Mary's, Isles of Scilly', *Cornish Archaeology,* No.32, 1993

Grundy, Mark, 'The Martello Towers of Minorca', *Fort,* No.4, 1990

Harris, Dr Edward, 'The Martello Tower at Ferry Point, St. Georges' Island, Bermuda', *Mariner's Mirror,* Vol.74, No.2, May 1988

Haslam, Charlotte, 'Landmarks in Coastal Defence', *Fortress,* No.4, Feb.1990

Kerrigan, Paul M., 'Minorca and Ireland, an Architectural Connection: the Martello Towers of Dublin Bay', *Irish Sword,* Vol.15, 1983

-, 'The Defences of Ireland. 2: The Martello Towers', *An Cosantoir* (Journal of the Irish Defence Force), May, 1974

Lewis, Col. George, RE, 'Report on the Application of Forts, Towers and Batteries to Coast Defences and Harbours', *Professional Papers of the Royal Engineers,* Vol.VII, 1844

-, 'Some Account of the Field Works Thrown up for the Defence of Sicily in 1810', *Professional Papers of the Royal Engineers,* Vol.III (New Series)

Mead, Cdre H.P., RN, 'The Martello Towers of England', *Mariner's Mirror,* Vol.34, 1948

Naval Chronicle, 'Biographical Memoir of Admiral Sir Charles Knowles, Bt, RN', Vol.II, 1799

O'Brien, Comdt B.M., 'Martello Towers', *An Cosantoir* (Journal of the Irish Defence Force), July 1965

Pegden, Brian K., 'The Purchase of Bricks for Martello Towers in the Year 1804', *Fort,* Vol.8, 1980

-, 'Martello Towers and Related Works (an Introduction to Published Material and Official Records)', *Ravelin* (Journal of the Kent Defence Research Group), Nos. 42, 44, 45, 46 and 49, 1995-96

Pocock, H.R.S., 'Jersey's Martello Towers', *Société Jersiaise Annual Bulletin,* 1971

V.H.C., 'The Brehon Tower', *Quarterly Review of the Guernsey Society,* Vol.VI, No.4, 1950-51

Walker, Kenneth, 'Martello Towers and the Defence of North East Essex in the Napoleonic War', *Essex Review,* Vol.47, 1938

Ward, S.G.P., 'Defence Works in Britain 1803-05', *Journal of the Society for Army Historical Research,* No.27, 1949

Glossary

Amusette	long-barrelled, small-calibre wall gun
Ashlar	square-hewn stones
Batter	backward slope of the surface of a wall
Barbette	position in which guns are mounted to fire over a parapet rather than through embrasures in the parapet wall
BL	breech-loading
Caponier	covered passage constructed across or projecting into, a ditch to provide sheltered communication across the ditch or to defend it
Carronade	large-calibre, short-barrelled gun
Coehorn	small, portable mortar
Corbel	projection of stone, timber, etc. jutting out from a wall to support its weight
Cordon	stone string course at the top or part way up a wall
Counterscarp	outer wall of a ditch
Counterscarp gallery	vaulted chamber constructed in the counterscarp in order to defend the ditch
Cunette	narrow moat in the middle of a dry ditch, built to improve drainage
Curtain	main wall of a fortified place which runs between the towers, bastions or gates

Embrasure   opening in a parapet or wall through which a gun can be fired

Glacis   open slope extending from the ditch giving a clear field of fire to the defenders

Keep   central tower of a fort or castle serving as a postion of last defence

Machicolation   gallery projecting from the wall of a tower with openings between the corbels through which fire can be brought on an enemy at the base of the tower

Parapet   stone breastwork designed to give the defenders on a wall or tower cover from fire and observation

Pas de souris   staircase giving access to a ditch

QF   quick-firing

Quatrefoil   four-cusped figure resembling a leaf with four branches (e.g., a four-leafed clover)

Racer   circular or semi-circular, horizontal metal rail along which the traversing platform of a heavy gun moves

Render (to)   to cover with a coat of plaster

RML   rifled muzzle loader: type of gun in use between 1850 and1890, just before the advent of modern breech-loading (BL) guns

Sallyport   passage giving access to the ditch for use by the defenders making a counterattack or sortie

SB   smooth-bore

Stucco   coarse plaster or cement used to cover the exterior surfaces of walls

Terreplein   area on top of a rampart or tower and surrounded by a parapet where guns are mounted

Tête de pont   fortification defending the approaches to a bridge

Trefoil   three-cusped figure resembling a leaf with three branches (e.g., a shamrock)

Wallpiece   small, muzzle-loading gun usually mounted on the wall of fortress and traversed by means of a swivel (sometimes called a swivel gun)

Index

Abercrombie Heights 124
Adam & Robertson 34
Admiralty, Board of 14-15, 27, 146
Alcock, Lt Alex., RA 68
Alde, River 36
Aldeburgh 16, 18, 25, 35-6, 45, 136, 145
Alderney 147
Allen, Lt William, RN 151
Anthony Hill 33, 41
Ascension Island 15, 151
Athlone 72, 145
Augusta 105, 108
Axe, War of, *see* Frontier War, 7th

Baginbun Head 27, 68-9
Ballinamuck 59
Baltic Association 93-4
Banagher 59, 72-3
Banc du Violet 88
Bantry Bay 13, 59, 61-2, 64, 68
Barbuda 122-4
Barrow's Hill 147
Bassett, Capt Frederick, RE 83, 86
Bayou Dupre 157
Bedford, Lt G.A., RN 151
Bennett, Capt William, RE 110
Bentinck, Maj-Gen Lord William 105, 109
Bere Island 13, 55-6, 61-2, 65-8
Berehaven 65
Bermuda 16, 22, 122, 126, 149
Bernard, Brig Gen Simon, USA 158
Bexhill 37, 40, 43
Birch, Capt John, RE 53, 55-6, 61, 65-7, 91-2, 162
Black River 117-19
Blanshard, Maj Thomas, RE 126, 149
Board of Ordnance 9, 14-15, 27-8, 31-2, 39, 61-2, 65, 67, 69, 70, 73, 87-8, 91-2, 94-5, 98,116-18, 122, 129, 136, 145-6,152, 153
Bois Blanc Island 152-3
Borgne, Lake 157-8
Brandreth, Capt Henry, RE 151
Bray 62
Brehon Rock 28
Bridges, Capt George, RE 113, 119, 150, 163
Brightlingsea 35, 47
Brown, Lt Col John, RE 32, 34
Brownrigg, Gen 31, 150
Brough, Lt Col Richard, RA 117
Bryce, Annan 82
Bryce, Lt Col Alexander, RE 91-2, 106, 129, 163
Buchanan, Lt Col Gilbert, RE 117
Bulverhythe 30, 37
Buzza 147

Cala San Esteve 53
Calder, Rear Adm Sir Robert, RN 65
Caleta de Fustes 50
Canary Islands 48, 50
Cape of Good Hope 101, 113, 115, 119, 142
Cape Town 113, 115, 162-3
Carleton 103
Carmichael-Smyth, Maj-Gen James, RE 138
Carmichael-Smyth Commission 138, 141,
Cashla Bay 72
Castillo de San Cristobel 48
Castlebar 59
Castlereagh, Viscount 101
Cathcart, Gen Lord 55, 61, 65-6
Ceylon 119, 150, 153
Charleston 155-6
Chateauguay 152
Chateau L'Etoc 147
Chatham, Earl of 14, 31-2, 36
Cherbourg 128, 134
Chippawa 153
Ciudadela 51, 53
Clacton-on-Sea 16, 18, 29, 47
Clinton, Col Henry 61
Coast Blockade 40, 44, 163
Coastguard, HM 37, 40, 47, 163
Cobbett, William 28
Cochrane, Capt Lord, RN 58, 67
Codrington, Sir William and Lady 122-3
Cole, Sir Lowry 117
Collingwood, Adm Lord, RN 105
Committee Drift 142
Committee of Engineers 14-15, 31, 34, 68, 70, 74, 78, 87, 99
Conway, Gen Seymore 83, 85-6
Coote, Sir Eyre 125
Cordiner, J. 119
Corfu 136-7
Cork (Harbour) 59, 61, 65, 76, 78-9, 145, 149
Cork District 67
Corsica 10, 30, 48, 61
Cowper, Capt Alex, BE 119
Craig, Lt Gen Sir James, 101, 113
Cramond Island 146
Croker, J.W. 94
Crockness 94
Cunningham, Lt Col Thomas, RE 117
Curzola 112

D'Arcy, Capt Robert, RE 53, 55, 162
Deben, River 29
DeButts, Capt Augustus, RE 61
Defence, Ministry of 37
Delhi 9, 120-2, 162
Delhi Gate 121
DeRullecourt, Baron 83, 87
DeVere, Maj Francis, RE 137
Director General of Artillery 131

Don, Lt-Gen Sir George 146
Doyle, Maj-Gen Sir John 12, 87, 147
Drogheda 62, 69
Dublin 13, 25, 27, 55, 59, 61-4, 68-9, 71, 81
Dumourriez, Gen 32
Dumplings Rocks 154
Duncannon 70, 73
Dundas, Maj-Gen David 12, 15, 30
Dungeness 34
Dunree 74
Dutton, Capt George, USA 159
Dymchurch 20, 27, 30, 33, 35-6, 43, 47, 65
Dyson, Lt George, RE 55, 61

Eastbourne 15, 18, 30, 33, 35, 37, 43, 47, 65
Eastern District 30
Eastern Cape Province 136, 142, 152, 162
East Essex Aviation Museum 47
Ecrehou Islands 146-7
Edinburgh 91
Edinburgh City Corporation 91-2, 146
English Heritage 47
Enniskillen 145
Elizabeth Castle 88
El Freus 51

Faro 106, 108
Faro Lines 106
Felixstowe 18, 40, 44
Fenian Brotherhood 79, 103
Fenwick, Lt-Col William, RE 67, 99, 152
Fermain Bay 146
Ferrara, Capt Francisco 106
Ferry Passage 126, 149
Fisher, Lt-Col Benjamin, RE 62, 70, 162
Folkestone 18, 24, 27, 30, 45, 47
Ford, Capt William, RE 10, 13, 15, 30, 163
Fornells 53, 57
Forts
    Adelaide 117
    Beaufort 142-3, 152
    Brown 142
    Castile, see Fort Nugent
    Charlotte 99
    Constitution (US) 155
    Denison 20, 143-4
    Down of Inch 75, 81
    Duncannon 73, 145
    East (Dunree) 75, 81
    Frederick 139
    George (Bermuda) 127
    George (Corfu) 136-7
    George (Mauritius) 117
    George (Minorca) 53
    George (Vis) 110-11
    Greencastle 76, 82
    Grey 87
    Henry 138, 141-2
    High Knoll 115

Houmet 87
Isabel II (Spanish) 57
Ladder Hill 115
Landguard 40
Marlborough 53
Nugent 125-6
Ostenburgh 150-1
Peddie 142
Picton 125
Regent 89, 146
Richmond 70
River   123
St. Blaise (Venetian) 112
St. Catherine 127
San Felipe (Spanish) 53
Saumaurez 87
Schulemburg (French) 136
Screven (US) 156
Snelling (US) 161
Thornton (Ascension) 151
Thornton (Sierra Leone) 116
Warburton (US) 155
Washington (US) 155
Wellington (Korcula) 112
Wellington (Vis) 112
West (Knockalla) 75
Westmoreland 78
Wetherill (US) 155
Yarmouth 149
Zachary Taylor (US) 159
Fort Point 27, 69
Fortitude, HMS 12
Freetown 115-16, 151
Fremantle 152
Fremantle, Rear-Adm Sir Thomas, RN
    109
Frontier War, 6th 142
    7th 143
Fuerteventura 50
Fyers, Maj-Gen William, RE 145

Galley Hill 27
Galway Bay 59, 70-1, 73
Gambia 151
Ganzirri 106-8
Garinish Island 13, 65, 68
Garrison 147
Georges Island 99
Glengarriff Harbour 65, 67, 82
Globsden Gut Sluice 35
Goffsett, Capt William, RE 39
Gogarty, Oliver St. John 82
Goper, Capt, RE 119
Gordon, Capt James, RN 155
Grahamstown 142, 152
Gran Canaria 48
Grand River North West 117-19
Grant Pass 157
Great Island 78-9

Great Yarmouth 145
Grouville Bay 83, 85-6

Halifax 95, 99, 101, 103-4, 114, 152, 154-6, 162
Hambantota 119
Hamilton, Sir William 106
Handfield, Maj John, RE 39
Hardwick, Lord 69
Harwich 29, 35, 40, 65
Hastings 30, 34
Havre des Pas 89
Heber, Bishop Reginald 121
Henryson, Capt John, RE 110, 113
Herm 135
Historic Scotland 94
Hobson, William 34
Hoche, Gen 59
Hodges, Edward 34
Hollesley Bay 29
Holloway, Maj Sir Charles, RE 65, 66, 68
Hood, Vice-Adm Lord, RN 150
Hoste, Capt George, RE 109
Hoste, Capt William, RN 109
Houmet de Longis 147
Howe, Adm Lord, RN 12
Hoy 94
Humbert, Gen 59, 74
Humfrey, Maj John, RE 84-5
Hunt, Capt Edward B., USA 159
Huron, Lake 152
Hythe 20, 32, 34, 41, 47
Hythe Division 37

Ile au Guerdain 87
Ile au Tonneliers 117
Iles Chaussey 146
Illnacullin 82
Imperieuse, HMS 58
Inch Island 74-5
Inchkeith 146
Inspector General of Fortifications 14, 34, 66-7, 71, 88, 92, 101, 130-1, 142
Ionian Islands 137
Ireland Island 149
Isla el Lazareto 51
Isle of Wight 149

Jackson Barracks 161
Jamaica 124-6
Jamestown 115
James Island (US) 155
James Joyce Museum 82
Jerbourg Peninsula 146
Jersey, Battle of 83
Jervois, Maj W.F., RE 133
Johnson, A.T.M. 46
Johnson, Sir Alexander 119
Jones, Col Sir John, RE 137
Joyce, James 82

Juliers 41
Juno, HMS 12

Keelogue 59, 127, 145-6
Kempt, Gen Sir James 88
Key, Capt Cooper, RN 133
Key West 159
Killalla 59
Kirkwall, Viscount 137
Kingston (Canada) 104, 136-40, 152-3, 161
Kingston (Jamaica) 125-6
Kinsale 145
Knowles, Capt Sir Charles, RN 122-3
Korcula *see* Curzola

Ladder Hill 115
Lake, Gen Lord 120
La Mola 51, 57-8
Langney Point 37
Lanzarote 50
Las Coloredas 50
Las Palmas 48
Lazareto 53
Le Hoche 74
Leith 91, 93, 146
Les Mielles de Morville 90
L'Etacq Point 88
Lewis, Col George, RE 88-9, 124, 142-3, 151, 153, 163
Linz 127
Lissa 109-13
Little Russel 135
Liverpool, Lord 109
Lomasney, William Francis 80
Londonderry 27, 74-5
Longhope Sound 22, 94
Long Lake 108
Long Mountain 125
Longy Bay 147
Lough Foyle 59, 70, 74, 76
Lough Swilly 57, 59, 70, 74-5, 82, 127
Louisiana 157
Lowen, Capt Pearce 112-13
Lowestoft 145
Lyman, Maj David, RA 147

Mackay, Capt *see* Lomasney, William Francis
Mackelcan, Capt John, RE 87
McNab Island 100
Magilligan Point 75-6
Magnisi 108
Mahebourg 117
Mahon 51, 55, 75
Mahratta War, 2nd 120
Maine 103
Maitland, Gen 150
Maitre Ile 147
Mann, Maj-Gen Gother, RE 71, 101

Mannez 147
Marino Point 79
Marmoutier 147
Marsh, Capt, RN 147
Marshland Sluice 35
Martello Towers
    Addaya 53-5, 58, 62
    Admiral Hood's   151
    Alcufar 53, 55, 58
    Aughinish 71
    Baginbun 69, 82
    Balbriggan 82
    Balcarrick 81
    Beacon Rock 92
    Belvelly 78
    Bentinck 110-11
    Brehon 133, 135
    Carleton 103
    Carriddi 108
    Cathcart 66-7, 81
    Cedar Island 139-40
    Clochlann 66
    Cole's 106
    Cork Abbey 80
    Craig's 113-15
    Cunningham 117-19
    Dalkey Island 63-4
    Drumanagh 81-2
    Duncannon 82
    Duke of Clarence 97-9, 104
    Duke of York 97-9, 104
    Dupre 157-8
    Dunree 57
    East 161
    East Branch Ditch 141
    Erskine 51, 53, 57-8
    Es Castell *see* Santandria
    Fanesker 73
    Ferry Point 127
    Finnavarra 71
    Fornells 53, 55, 57-8
    Fort Frederick 82, 139-40
    Fort Point 81
    Gando 48-9, 123
    Ganzirri 108
    General Brownrigg's 151
    Greencastle 82
    Hackness 94
    Hambantota 120
    Haulbowline 78, 82
    Howth 80
    Icho 87-8
    Ireland's Eye 63
    Kempt 22, 88, 90
    Knockalla 57, 75, 82
    La Collette 89-90
    La Preneuse 118-19
    Lazareto 55
    L'Etacq 89-90

Lewis 89-90
Los Freus *see* Erskine
Loughlinstown 81
Magilligan 77, 82
Magnisi 108
Maitland 136-7
Manly 81
Manning 79
Mount Stuart 53, 55, 58
Muckamish 82
Murney 139-41
North East 16, 28, 129, 131-2
Paget's 106
Penjat *see* Mount Stuart
Phillipet 53-4, 58
Pointe de l'Harmonie 119
Portelet 87
Portmarnock 81
Prince of Wales 95-8, 104, 154
Punta Prima 53, 55, 58
Rambla *see* Sa Torreta
Red Island 81
Ringaskiddy 78
Rossaveel 72
Robertson 110
Robswall 81
Rossleague 78-9
Rush 81
Sa Mesquita 53, 56, 58, 75
Sa Nitja 53, 58
Sa Torreta 51, 53, 58
St. Clair 51, 53, 57-8
St. David *see* Fort Picton
St. Nicholas 51, 53
Sandycove 64, 82
Sandymount 63, 82
Santandria 54, 56-8
Sargantana Island 53-4, 57-8
Seapoint 82
Sherbrooke 99, 104
Shoal 139-40
Simon's Town 113-15, 120
Son Bou 58
South West 28, 129, 131-2
Spit of Grain 134-5
Stack Rock 132, 134, 149
Sutton Creek 81
Tour de Vinde 87
Tybee island 156
Union 116
Victoria 89-90
Walbach 155
West 160
West Branch Ditch 141
Williamstown 63, 82
Wish 43
Master General of the Ordnance 14, 66,
    88, 92, 101, 117
Mauritius 16, 117-18

Maximilian, Archduke 128
Mazzone Canal 108
Medway 133-4
Meelick 59, 72-3
Messina 105-6
Metcalfe, Sir Charles 121
Milazzo 105-6
Milford Haven 28, 128-9, 132-3,135, 149
Millmount Hill 70
Minneapolis 161
Minorca 12, 22, 24, 48, 50, 61, 64, 67,
    83, 105, 113, 142, 162
Mobile Bay 158
Moira, Lord 146
Mount Orgueil Castle 89
Mortella Point 12, 30, 48, 51
Morse, Maj Gen Robert, RE 31-2, 34, 68,
    71, 92
Mournes Hill 145
Muckamish Point 74-5
Mulcaster, Capt Frederick, RE 86, 142-3, 152
Murat, Marshal 105

Naples, Kingdom of 105
Napoleon I 28-9, 147, 158
Napoleon III 158
Narragansett Bay 154
Neid's Point 74
Nepean, Lt-Col Thomas, RE 15
New Brunswick 102-3
New Hampshire 155
New Orleans 158, 161
New Romney 43
Newford Down 147
Newhaven (Sussex) 15
Niagara 138, 152-3
Noirmont Point 87
Normans Bay 27, 46
Nun's Island 152

Oldfield, Lt-Col John, RE 152
Ontario, Lake 136, 138
Ore, River 36
'Oregon crisis' 139, 153
Orford Haven 35
Orkney 22, 94
Orwell, River 18, 29, 40
Otway, Caesar 68, 82
Oysterhaven 145

Pasley, Lt Charles, RE 53, 55-7, 163
Pass au Heron 157-8
Peacock, USS 143
Pembroke Dock 16, 28, 128-32, 140, 149
Peninnis 147
Peto, Harold 82
Petts Level 27
Phillipet Peninsula 51
Picton, Lt-Col Thomas 124

Pinchgut Island 143-4
Pitt, Rt Hon. William 31-2
Playa Blanca 50
Point Levi 152-3
Pointe des Pas 89
Pompee, HMS 109
Port Louis 117
Port of Spain 124, 149
Porto San Giorgio 110-11
Portsmouth (US) 155
Potomac River 155
Prince Edward, HRH 95-6
Privy Council 31
Proctor's Landing 158

Quebec 101-2, 138, 152, 162
Queenborough 147
Queenborough Lines 147
Queenston Heights 153

Ramsey, Col, RE 125
Raz Island *see* Houmet de Longis
Redoubts
    Drop 33
    Duke of Clarence 97
    Duke of York 97, 100
    Dymchurch 47
    Eastbourne 41, 47
    Harwich 47
    Napoleon (French) 136
    Packenham 145
    Signal (French) 136
Regiments
    Infantry
        11th Royal Veteran Bn 27
    Royal Artillery
        64 Fd Regt 43
        552 Coast Defence Regt 43
Rennie, John 34
Rerrin 66
Reynolds, Maj Thomas 30
Rhode Island 154
Richlieu River 138, 152
Rideau Canal 138-9
Ringaskiddy Hill 78
Robertson, Lt-Col George 110, 112
Rochester Conference 31-4
Romney Marsh 34, 39
Rosslare Point 68, 81
Round Lake 108
Rowley, Capt Sir Charles, RN 109
Royal Carriage Department 131, 140
Royal Engineers 14, 15, 20, 41, 118, 146
Royal Military Canal 34-6, 39
Royal Military College of Canada 140
Rye 18-19, 27, 30, 32-3, 37, 40

Sackets Harbor 138
Saint Charles River 152

Saint John 102-3
St. Agata 106-7
St. Aubin's Bay 88
St. Catherine's Bay 85
St. Clement's Bay 87
St. George's Island 126-7, 149
St. Helena 115
St. Helier 83, 146
St. John's 152-3
St. Lawrence River 138
St. Mary's 147
St. Osyth 47
St. Ouen's Bay 85, 89
Sandgate Castle 16, 33
Sandymount 62
Santandria 57
Sargantana Island 53
Savannah 155
Saxe, Marshal 10, 30, 73
Scilly Isles 147
Sea Fencibles 62, 147
Seaford 15-16, 18, 47
Shah Jahan, Emperor 120
Shahjahanabad 120
Shannon, River 59, 70-1, 73, 127, 145
Shannonbridge 59, 72
Sheerness 28, 133, 147
Sheffield, Lord 61
Sherbrooke, Lt-Gen Sir John 100
Shipley, Brig-Gen Sir Thomas, RE 125-6, 149
Shorncliffe 18, 24, 34, 37, 41, 45
Sicily 16, 105, 108-10
Sierra Leone 115-16, 151
Sierra Leone Company 115, 151
Simcoe, Lt-Gen John 147
Smith, John 34
Smith, Capt Henry, RN 108
Smith, Col Richard Baird, RE 121
South Carolina 155
Southern District 10, 15, 30
Spike Island 78
Spit of Grain 28, 133-5
Sri Lanka see Ceylon
Stack Rock 28, 129
Stour, River 40
Stuart, Lt-Gen Sir Charles 51, 106
Sutcliffe, Sheila 41
Sutton Creek 61
Sydney 143-4
Syracuse 105, 108

Tarbert 145
Tenerife 50
Tombeau Bay 117
Tone, Wolfe 59
Totten, Lt Col Joseph G., USA 158
Tours Modeles 153-8
Towers
    Archirondel 85

'Corsican' 69
Cromwell's 73
'Geneose' 10
'Hammer' 12
La Rocco 85, 89
Malakoff 128
Maximilian 56
Mont Crevelt 86
Pelorus 106
'Picket' 142-3
Rousse 86
'Saracen' 10
Seymour 83, 85, 87
Tower Hill (Jersey) 146
Tower Hill (Sierra Leone) 115-16
Trinidad 124, 162
Trumpeter's Drift   142
Twiss, Brig-Gen William, RE 10, 13,
    15, 30-2, 34, 59, 64, 71, 74, 162
Tybee Island 155

United Irishmen 59
United States Navy Exploring 143
    Expedition

Vido 136-7
Vincennes, USS 143
Vis see Lissa
Vulliamy, Justin 46

Walbach, John 155
Walsh, Capt Thomas 53
Walton Ferry 18
Walton-on-the-Naze 18
Wansey Hill 116
War Department 40, 44, 47, 81, 137
Ward, Ronald 44
Waterford 73
Watts, Lt-Col Henry, RE 150-1
Wellesley, Sir Arthur see Wellington,
    Duke of
Wellington, Duke of 14, 69, 138
Wellington Lunette 136-7
Western District 147
Western Heights 33
Wexford 62
Whiddy Island 65, 68
Whitmore, Lt-Col George, RE 137,
    163
Whitshed, Rear-Adm James, RN 62
Wickham, Rt Hon. William 62, 65
Wilkes, Lt Charles, USN 143
Willop Sluice 35
Worsley, Lt, RE 136-7

Xhosa 142-3, 152

York, HRH Duke of 29, 31
Yorke, Rt Hon. Charles 109
Youghal 145